A colour guide to
RARE WILD FLOWERS

D0503439

A colour guide to
RARE WILD FLOWERS

John Fisher

Constable · London

First published in Great Britain 1991
by Constable and Company Limited
3 The Lanchesters, 162 Fulham Palace Road
London W6 9ER
Copyright © 1991 by John Fisher
The right of John Fisher to be identified
as the author of this Work has been
asserted by him in accordance with the
Copyright, Designs and Patents Act 1988
ISBN 0 09 469190 8 (PVC)
ISBN 0 09 470780 4 (Hardback)
Set in Monophoto 9pt Photina by
Servis Filmsetting Limited, Manchester
Printed in Great Britain by
BAS Printers Limited,
Over Wallop, Hampshire

A CIP catalogue record for this book
is available from the British Library

Contents

Acknowledgements

Many of the photographs in this miscellany would never have materialised without help and encouragement from like-minded botanists who have supported the conception and execution of this Guide, and assisted in its formulation. I am permanently grateful to them all for their tolerance and forbearance on so many arduous and exacting occasions.

How to use this guide

For convenience, the most productive areas for rare wild flowers in Britain have been arranged in seven Groups:

One   *The Home Counties*, including the Thames Valley, the North and South Downs, the New Forest and the Isle of Wight.
Two   *The West Country*, including Dorset, Wiltshire, Avon. Somerset, Devon and Cornwall.
Three   *The Isles of Scilly*.
Four   *East Anglia*, including Essex, Cambridgeshire, Suffolk, Norfolk and Lincolnshire.
Five   *Wales*, including Snowdonia, Anglesey, Great Orme, Brecon, Powys and the Gower Peninsula.
Six   *North of England*, including Derbyshire, Lancashire, Yorkshire, Co. Durham, Northumbria and Cumbria.
Seven   *Scotland*, including Tayside, Highlands and the Isle of Skye.

The plants within each of these seven areas are arranged in the alphabetical order of their 'English' names, as adopted in the *English Names of Wild Flowers* by J.G. Dony, F.H. Perring and C.M. Rob, published by the Botanical Society of the British Isles.

Each page of the text carries a miniature map of the area to which it refers.

For ready reference, the Guide also contains an index of both the botanical and vernacular names of the plants described.

This book is written on the premise that the closer individuals come to seeing and identifying rare wild plants, the more concerned they will become to protect them and to leave them for others to enjoy.

However, as a measure of protection, the locations of some of the rarer plants are sketched here only in outline and I regret that I cannot answer requests for further details.

NOTE

Plants marked with an asterisk are those legally protected in England, Scotland and Wales under the Wildlife and Countryside Act of 1981 and its amendments.

AREA ONE: HOME COUNTIES

1: *Thames Valley*

Birthwort (*Aristolochia clematitis*)

A pilgrimage to the ruins of Godstow nunnery in Oxfordshire to see this extremely rare plant is well worth the time spent, especially as the flowers are normally on show more or less continuously between June and September.

The ancient nunnery can be conveniently reached after driving little more than half a mile from the city of Oxford, taking the A34 road northwards, and branching off on to a country lane to the left.

Do not, though, hope to find Birthwort climbing up the crumbling walls of the ruin itself. Look, rather, on the banks of the ditches bordering the neighbouring meadows where the plant sprawls, head-high and more, across the surrounding vegetation. Its large, heart-shaped leaves are dull green, and the pale yellow flowers are scattered in small bunches lying partly concealed beneath the leaves.

For centuries Birthwort was taken, as a decoction or steeped in wine, to ensure a smooth and painfree delivery and to quell the pangs of after-birth. To wise men – and the old wives – of the past, the flowers of Birthwort, when pointing downwards, as they do when fully developed, displayed a basal swelling with a narrow tube beneath, reminiscent of the womb and the canal leading downwards from it: features which were interpreted as a sign from heaven enjoining mankind to utilise the virtues of this unusual plant. Presumably the nuns of Godstow used the plant in the Infirmary which they ran for the benefit of local villagers.

*Downy Woundwort (*Stachys germanica*)

This splendid plant – another Oxfordshire treasure – needs to be
sharply distinguished from the garden bed-filler Lambs' Ears *Stachys
byzantina* – sometimes *Stachys lanata* – which sends out branches
sprawling in all directions. Our wild plant rises up unbranched, and
pointing to the heavens as surely as a church spire. The whole plant
is covered with soft, silky hairs – giving it a 'dusty miller' look
unmatched by the denizens of the flower-bed. The lipped tubular
flowers, of a sharp purplish pink, are disposed on whorls around the
stem.

Downy Woundwort seems particularly to favour old Roman roads
(as, for example Akerman Street) and is closely associated with the
so-called 'green lanes', namely those with wide verges bounded by
hedges, along which drovers once travelled with their herds. Indeed
it has been suggested that the tramping of the Roman legions and
the subsequent passage of the drovers and their carts may have
broken up the soil and cleared away the competing vegetation in a
way that allowed buried seeds of Downy Woundwort to germinate.

Plants have been reported somewhat unpredictably from at least
eleven sites, mainly within a small area around a line drawn
between Witney and Charlbury. Four of these sites have recently
been active. A search along the borders of the green lanes in the
designated area, especially those in which the hedges have been cut
and the scrub cleared, offers the best chance of meeting this
extremely rare species. Look for a plant about 2 feet high, in July.

Dragon's Teeth (*Tetragonolobus maritimus*)

The best-known Dragon's Teeth were those sown by Cadmus, the fabled Phoenician who presented Greece with its first alphabet. The 'teeth' grew up into a crop of armed men who all but killed Cadmus himself. Even today, the ivory-coloured flowers, massed together, do suggest a flashback to, if not a repetition of, the myth.

The plant grows wild in Greece – and elsewhere across the Mediterranean – but in Britain the species, though well established, is still regarded as alien. It grows to a respectable height of 9 or 10 inches, and is easily distinguished by the solitary yellow flowers and, later, by its four-angled, winged pods.

Dragon's Teeth thrives in rough grassland on chalk or gravel, often on sites near the sea, as for instance at Hockley, a suburb of Southend, and at West Mersea. There are eight sites in Kent, spread out along or near the southern shore of the Thames estuary. But a well-known and more centrally placed site is in Buckinghamshire, to the east of the village of Fingest, south-west of High Wycombe, on an approximate grid reference of 786-916. Here, on a broad 'island' between the road and the hedge, the plants grow in profusion, as they do also further uphill on the bend of the lane leading towards Fingest Grove. Admittedly this site is hardly a maritime one, being more than 60 miles from the nearest sea-shore, and there have been suggestions that the local authority may have restocked some of their wayside verges with seed imported from France. All summer.

*Fringed Gentian (*Gentianella ciliata*)

To visit this recently (1982) rediscovered rarity, we shall be standing on a gentle slope near Wendover on the northern escarpment of the Chilterns, looking closely at the downland turf, hunting for the flowers of the Fringed Gentian. They are deep purple, and up to $1\frac{1}{2}$ inches across. When open, the long, narrow petals are disposed windmill-fashion, like the four blades of a purple propeller, and each has along its edges a white silken fringe, the 'eye-lash' which gives the plant both its English and its botanical name. On dull days when the petals close, folded across each other and wrapped together like a furled umbrella, only one white fringe, the longer of the two on that petal, is visible.

The plant was discovered by a Miss M. Williams, out for a walk near Wendover one autumn day in 1875. She thought her find was Marsh Gentian. Nothing further was heard of the Fringed Gentian in England till the summer of 1982, when P. Phillipson discovered an unfamiliar plant also on chalk grassland near Wendover. It was one of a lively colony of more than 40 Fringed Gentian plants growing within each reach of two public footpaths. Since then, plans have been made for a warden to watch over the plants during their mid-September flowering season.

*Ghost Orchid (*Epipogium aphyllum*)

The Ghost Orchid is well named. With its leafless stalk and flowers of pallid white, it haunts the shadows of the darkest beechwoods, and is unpredictable in its appearances.

The petals and sepals are in two whorls, outer and inner, and, with the exception of the one which forms the lip, droop downwards in confusion. The lip, however, unlike those of most orchids, is thrown upwards, giving the impression of a sun-bonnet. Behind it, also pointing upwards, is a short blunt spur, suggesting the head of the bonnet-wearer.

The Ghost Orchid may appear in any given year, at any time between June and September, depending on the amount of moisture available in the soil during the spring months when the needs of the plant for nourishment would be at their greatest.

Two of the modern sites were found in the 1920s and '30s near Henley-on Thames, Oxfordshire by Mrs Vera Paul, then a schoolgirl. Two more Chiltern sites have since been found, the most productive (24 plants on one occasion) lying in the smaller Buckinghamshire woods to the west of Marlow. Almost certainly there are other sites to be revealed in the Chiltern beechwoods. For no matter how overcast the day, the beech leaves, curled a myriad different ways, will snatch the light from the sky overhead and transform it into dozens of reflections, any of which could be the plant itself.

Meadow Clary (*Salvia pratensis*)

Here is a splendid, outstandingly beautiful species which towers a yard or more high above the July herbage, and in some cases obliges the sightseer by growing on roadside verges.

It should first be distinguished from its humbler cousin, Wild Clary, the flowers of which are seldom more than ⅜ inch long and are sometimes shorter than the surrounding calyx in which they are cupped.

Meadow Clary is not only a rare species but is regarded as highly vulnerable. It is conspicuous; it is attractive enough to lure 'collectors'; and many of the colonies are enclosed on private estates which, strange to say, makes them in some cases more difficult to protect than if they were in the open countryside. The plants seem to thrive on land that is disturbed by vehicles – even tanks – and grazed by rabbits. Look in June and July.

Oxfordshire is the true home of the Meadow Clary, and one of the surest ways of seeing a display of the plants is, in this year of writing, to take the B4022 road northwards from Charlbury (locally pronounced Chorlbury). Drive with caution and survey the right-hand side of the road, going north. After less than 1¼ miles you could begin to see stands of Meadow Clary. More plants are visible further north along the right-hand side of the B4022 up to the point where a rough and ready track, known as the Saltway but rarely so named on maps, crosses the B4022 from north-west to south-east. Turn left here and continue along the Saltway on foot.

Pasque Flower (*Pulsatilla vulgaris*)

This wild Pasque Flower was photographed in Gloucestershire, one sunny 4 May.

Pasque Flowers hold their beauty from the moment of birth till long after their purple 'petals' (they are in fact sepals) have been shed. At first all that can be seen are the grape-coloured buds hugging the turf – date-shaped but clothed with the finest silky hair. Next, the tips of the 'petals', each curling outwards, can be distinguished, and the flowers rise up, pointing to the sky. Later the golden stamens appear, the inner rings providing pollen, the outer rings nectar.

The downs to the north-east of Cirencester are the most westerly site for the Pasque Flower, and support what is probably the largest colony in the whole of the UK. The plants are on private land, suitably remote from the road, and permission to visit them should be obtained from the owner through the Gloucester Naturalists' Society (see Appendix for the addresses of local Wildlife Trusts).

Alternative sites are the chalk downland of Therfield Heath in Hertfordshire near Royston, on the Devil's Dyke earthwork south-west of Newmarket, and even within the reserve midway between Peterborough and Stamford, which is inelegantly named Hills and Holes.

Spring Crocus (*Crocus vernus*)

The wise men have clearly been perplexed as to the right name for this member of the Iris family, and some have called it Purple Crocus (*Crocus purpureus*). There is something to be said, however, for the name Spring Crocus because there is another naturalised purple Crocus (*C. nudiflorus*) which flowers in the autumn.

The Spring Crocus, as we shall call it, is the plant to be seen flowering in profusion amid the melting snows of the Alps. It was a popular importation among gardeners of the sixteenth century but may have been brought here originally by the Crusaders. Since then it has managed to establish itself permanently in the wild in a few undisturbed old meadows and pastures in both Wales (Glamorgan, Dyfed and Clwyd) and parts of Scotland and Ireland.

However, the most famous wild crocus meadow in the country has been bought (1986) and is managed by the Berkshire, Buckinghamshire and Oxfordshire Naturalists' Trust (BBONT) at Inkpen. Even in February the meadow is streaked with thousands of purple flowers – and some white forms too. Records show that crocuses have been flowering there since 1800, but do not relate how they first appeared.

The site is conveniently reached by taking the A4 road westwards from Newbury towards Hungerford and crossing the River Kennet at Kintbury. In Inkpen, make for Pottery Lane. Between houses in Pottery Lane there is an inconspicuous track, the opening to which is marked with a BBONT Reserve sign. The gate into the meadow is less than 100 yards up this track. Dogs on leads, please.

Summer Snowflake (*Leucojum aestivum*)

Surely no rare wild flower could be nearer the centre of the Thames Valley than this one. For its alternative 'English' synonym, Loddon Lily, refers to one of the tributaries of the Thames along which it loves to grow. This plant thrives on ground that has been flooded during the winter; flowers appear in April and May.

There is a good site for Summer Snowflake on Andersey Island (which can be reached dry-shod from Abingdon), and two other sites either side of the bridge a few miles east at Clifton Hampden, where the author Robert Gibbings, exploring the Thames in a flat-bottomed boat, counted 128 House Martin nests built in the arches of the bridge. There are other sites either side of Shillingford Bridge.

There are also clumps along the towpath on the east side of the river from Wargrave towards Temple Combe, on the reach from Henley to Remenham, and between Hurley and Bisham. Other localities easily reached on foot are in the Wokingham area – near Sandford Bridge and on the east side of the River Loddon south of Loddon Bridge.

Some sites can be reached only from a boat, and permission should be sought before going ashore or even when mooring alongside the bank. Trespassing is to avoided at all costs. Indeed, provoking farmers or landowners along the Thames and its tributaries could put the survival of the plants at risk.

Wild Tulip (*Tulipa sylvestris*)

The flowers of the Wild Tulip are brilliant yellow, with rather loosely arranged pointed petals marked on the reverse with a faint green stripe. They are carried on stems up to 2 feet high – fairly tall as tulips go. They are quite distinct from the plethora of cultivars of different heights, shapes and colours offered by commercial growers. At some nurseries the wild species is on sale in its own right.

The flower shown here could well be the descendant of the original tulip from which all garden species sprang for, as yet, no one has succeeded in discovering the wild form of the red *Tulip gesnerana* which was the first garden tulip ever to have been introduced into Europe. In Britain, from the type of places in which it flowers – old orchards, undisturbed meadows and hedgerows – the Wild Tulip is assumed to have been introduced.

In the Thames Valley, the best-known site is a small field next to the Village Hall in West Challow, Oxfordshire, 2 miles west of Wantage. The villagers are proud of their treasure, and the lady with grazing rights over the field (which appears to have been ploughed at some time in the past) forbears to turn her ponies out to grass until flowering is over, usually before mid-May.

An alternative site is to be found at Harefield in Middlesex, 3 miles south of Rickmansworth. Some good specimens of the Wild Tulip are to be found there in a small copse behind the church.

Winter Aconite (*Eranthis hyemalis*)

'Winter' is the right word for this plant, as it is often in flower in January, sometimes under a cover of snow. It has, too, some features in common with another Aconite, the dark violet Monk's-hood, since both belong to the Buttercup family and both contain an alkaloid poison.

Winter Aconite is given the highest rarity rating of three 'stars' in that much-treasured *Pocket Guide* by David McClintock and R.S.R. Fitter. Other works treat it as widely naturalised in parks and gardens. So perhaps we could compromise by agreeing that it is very seldom seen in the wild. The plants grow to 4 or 5 inches and each bears a single globe-like bloom: an orb made up of six golden sepals, for the plant has no petals. Three dark green, deeply slashed stem-leaves grow immediately beneath each flower, to form a kind of 'bib'.

There are two accessible sites in the Thames Valley. One is around the moat beneath the Round Tower in Windsor Castle, reached after a short walk from the Castle Gate. The other involves some motoring, albeit through delightful country, to the village of Swyncombe in Oxfordshire. In February almost half of the churchyard is lit with gold.

More recently gardeners have been turning away from Winter Aconite to grow the rather similar but larger-flowered species *Eranthis cilicica*. If this trend continues, the original Winter Aconite could eventually become as rare in gardens as it is already outside them.

*Yellow Star-of-Bethlehem (*Gagea lutea*)

We are perhaps stretching a point in characterising this rare plant as a speciality of the Thames Valley, though one of its finest colonies lines the bank of the Evenlode, a tributary of the Thames. The plants, widely and sparsely scattered as they are, seem particularly at home when surrounded by stone walls, and a flourishing colony is to be found at Thrift Wood, Cleeve Hill, near the highest point of the Cotswolds.

A second, easily reached site exists in the West Country not far to the south of Junction 18 of the M4. Taking the A46 in the direction of Bath, we pass two crossroads, the second of which is signposted to the village of West Littleton, a mere 5 miles from Badminton. Look for a small sliver of woodland within the south-west quadrant of the crossroads. The flowers should be on show during the second week of April.

Seen in isolation, when not closely surrounded by Dog's Mercury, the Yellow Star-of-Bethlehem is an arresting plant with its single large hooded leaf arching away from the main stem like a green water-spout, and its flower-stalks sprouting from almost the same spot on the main stem. The narrow petals however eventually curve backwards; their yellow colours fade all too soon. The plant is really at its best before the flowers have become star-like, while the green banding on the reverse of the petals is still there to suggest a new curtain fabric or wallpaper design.

2: North and South Downs

Bastard-Toadflax (*Thesium humifusum*)

How did this member of the Sandalwood family come by its uncomplimentary name, since the flowers look nothing like those of a Toadflax? Probably because its leaves reminded earlier botanists of those of the Toadflaxes (which in turn had been dubbed Toadflax because they were not from the same botanical 'family' as the true Flaxes – although the leaves of the two species are similar).

Bastard-Toadflax grows on short-grassed chalk downland and is becoming progressively more rare with the decline of the rabbit population on the one hand and the proliferation of developers on the other.

Most of the locations are in southern counties, though it appears to have vanished from Somerset and Kent, as well as from Glamorgan except as a casual. It remains in Gloucestershire, as for instance on Barnsley Warren, north-east of Cirencester, and in Surrey on downs westwards from Purley and Riddlesdown. It occurs on the Isle of Wight on Freshwater Downs, in Hampshire on Farley Mount Country Park and in Wiltshire on Pewsey and Wylye Down. Sussex, however, is the most favoured county. In the west, it grows on the downland within Arundel Park, and on Mount Caburn, 2 miles east of Lewes. It occurs again on the downs rising to the east of Cuckmere Haven and further east still on the short turf above Beachy Head. It flowers from June throughout the summer.

Burnt Orchid (*Orchis ustulata*)

A hooded petal of dark maroon completely covers each of the buds of this rare and decorative little orchid, so that when coming into flower, the upper part of the spike fully lives up to its 'English' name.

Its life-cycle is one of the slowest in the orchid family. The rootstock develops underground with the aid of a beneficial fungus for as long as 15 years before the first leaf pierces the ground. A few more years roll by before the first flowers appear. During the whole of this period, the ground must remain undisturbed.

The largest colonies of Burnt Orchid plants in the UK are in Wiltshire. Several hundred plants have been counted within the Great Cheverell Nature Reserve, near the village of that name, and either side of Tilshead, further south along the A360. Clearbury Ring, to the west of the A338, is another well established site.

Further north two ancient earthworks at Milk Hill and Adam's Grave about 4 miles south of East Kennett have defied the plough. In Kent, there are some, but not many plants in the reserve managed by the Kent Trust for Nature Conservation at Queensdown Warren near Stockbury.

Most colonies flower in late May but a few regularly favour July. The flowers are said, by one respected botanist, to smell of stewed cherries.

Coralwort (*Cardamine bulbifera*)

At first it looks like the much commoner Lady's Smock *Cardamine pratensis*, that milky-mauve-flowered plant of the water-meadows much beloved by Orange-Tip butterflies. However, the main stem-leaves of the Lady's Smock are pinnate, with narrow leaflets arranged on either side of a central stalk, whereas the middle stem-leaves of the Coralwort are divided into three equal parts.

The Coralwort, or Coralroot as some people prefer to call it, earned its name from the complex formation of the white underground stem, which to earlier botanists suggested sections of a reef. It is stated unequivocally to be a native species, although in our climate it rarely casts any seed. Instead, it reproduces itself from bulbils – small, dark purple, almost black 'bulbs', formed above ground in the axils of the leaves.

Coralwort is found in two widely separated areas, and in two different habitats. In the Chilterns it must be sought in the chalkland beechwoods lying between Hughenden Valley and Saunderton in Buckinghamshire. This is the kind of habitat in which it grows on the continent of Europe. The other favoured area is south of the Thames along the north-eastern border of Sussex and in copses just across the Kent side. There is one other site in Sussex, but on chalk, near Rake, just on the Sussex side of the border with Hampshire. This site, on a crossroads, is ominously near a road-maintenance lay-by, but, in the years since the plants were first noticed there, they have been spreading freely into the beechwoods around. Mid-April is the time to be looking.

*Cut-leaved Germander (*Teucrium botrys*)

This is by far the most decorative among the wild Germanders of Britain, although the whole plant is often no more than 3 inches tall. The leaves are pinnatifid, that is with leaflets arranged in two rows along a common stalk, but with lobes connected together by tissue as well as along a common midrib. The bracts surrounding the flowers are also pinnatifid and the flowers, in whorls along the branches, are pinkish-purple.

The species occurs only on chalk, particularly on grassland, or on fields that have been left fallow. One locality exists in Gloucestershire in the Daneway Nature Reserve (permit only) where special efforts are made to encourage the plants by loosening the soil in the area around which they might be expected to seed.

In Kent, a site has been known for nearly a century on downland and in a chalk pit at Upper Halling, south-west of Rochester. There is also a traditional site on chalk-spoil heaps near Micheldever in Hampshire, where the soil was disturbed during the earlier development of the railway. An attempt to introduce the plant to Headley Warren in Surrey has, however, been regarded with some disfavour, since the Nature Conservancy Council normally approves of reintroductions or restocking only where a rare plant has recently become extinct or is on the verge of extinction in an area which is still apparently suitable for it, or can be made so, and provided with some long-term protection. Mid July is best.

Drooping Star-of-Bethlehem (*Ornithogalum nutans*)

In 1548 William Turner admitted in his pioneering work *The Names of Herbes*: 'I can not tel howe that it is called in englishe for I neuer sawe it in Englande, sauying onely besyde Shene herde by the Temmes syde.' John Gerard who kept a garden himself in Holborn seems to have been the first to use the name Star-of-Bethlehem. So we may assume that this is an introduced plant that has spread to the wild from gardens and orchards.

The flowers are white, banded on the reverse with green, and are displayed in a short raceme – a flowering branch with new flowers continuing to grow at the end so that there is no obvious terminal flower. The flowers tend to point in one direction only.

Since the Drooping Star-of-Bethlehem is likely to be a relict of a garden or an escape from one, its appearance is somewhat unpredictable. There are records of it from the roadside verge at Bromsberrow in Gloucestershire as well as from Tunstall and Great Bealings churchyard in Suffolk. Another site is in Hampshire near Selborne. A group of plants has taken position at the top of a tall bank, not by any means close to houses or gardens. The route runs eastward from Selborne as far as Oakwood Farm where there is a turn to the left. The plants are roughly half-way down the lane towards Oakhanger Farm on the right-hand side at approximately grid reference SU 770–350.

This is an early budding plant with flowers to be expected at the end of March or the beginning of April.

Green Hellebore (*Helleborus viridis*)

Dish-like, light green flowers and sword-like leaflets make this one of the showiest wild plants – and one of the earliest. The normal date for flowers in the south of England is during the second or third week of February, in the north perhaps several weeks later. The leaves are not on show during the winter.

It loves an alkaline soil, and occurs on carboniferous limestone as far north as Lancashire and on the magnesian and oolite limestone of Yorkshire. It prefers woods with trees that shed their leaves in winter, so that early spring sunshine can reach the plants beneath. It is best suited by woods that are damp and sheltered from the summer sun by a canopy of leaves, so that a modicum of moisture remains throughout the dry season. Consequently, when trees are felled and the ground around them is left unprotected, the plants eventually die out.

Among the sites that have survived, after a fashion, is one in the beechwoods of Duncton to the south of Petworth in West Sussex, where two rides cross at an approximate grid reference of SU 967-145. Other sites exist in woods further west along the Hampshire border. Further investigation is needed of sites such as Wick Wood at Selborne in Hampshire, Hurdleshaw Wood near Streatley in Oxfordshire, and Thorpe near Ashbourne in Derbyshire, where the flowers have been known traditionally.

Ground Pine (*Ajuga chamaepitys*)

This plant does indeed resemble a small pine seedling, but one permanently confined to ground level. It is said to smell of pine when crushed, which is not surprising since it belongs to the same family group as marjoram and the mints.

This is an extremely local plant more or less confined to the chalk downs of south-eastern counties of England, and, being an annual, it springs up most frequently on ground that has been disturbed where, in consequence, there is reduced competition from the perennials. Thus chalk arable fields are the most likely sites for the Ground Pine, and, though it flowers almost continuously from May through to September, the best time to look for it is after the corn has been harvested.

In Kent it is present, very locally, in 13 locations, the majority on chalk fields and downs above the west bank of the River Medway, particularly in areas disturbed by rabbits. One good site lies in the semi-industrial neighbourhood of Cuxton, not far from Rochester. But along the North Downs, Surrey offers the best chances to the botanist. Ground Pine has been found in ploughed fields below Hackhurst Downs, above Gomshall near Dorking on an approximate grid reference of 100-485, as well as on disturbed ground by a motor road near Headley, 3 miles east of Leatherhead. Elsewhere in Surrey it has been found in places where the chalk has been dug up for pipe-laying, a not infrequent occurrence in this fast-developing county.

Lady Orchid (*Orchis purpurea*)

This is notionally the elder sister of the Burnt Orchid, shown opposite page 44, and it would be no surprise to find a specimen standing 2 feet high – double the size of its smaller relative.

The flowers – up to fifty on a single spike – are each crowned with a helmet of petals, at first almost black, but later dark purple or even darkest red. The lower lip of the orchid suggests a figure dressed in white satin flushed at the edges with pink and spotted with purple – just the sort of pattern that could be used for a lady's apron or crinoline, or even a divided skirt (for the lip is divided at the centre).

Kent is the acknowledged home for this species, and there are sites for it in clearings and open woods stretching from close to the western border of the county almost to Dover in the south-east and to the Isle of Grain in the north. The best fast-lane approach to this May-flowering orchid is through the Kent Trust for Nature Conservation (enclose a stamped and addressed envelope). The KTNC is one of the most active and informative of the Trusts, and has at least one good site in the Canterbury area which is wardened during the orchid's flowering season and is therefore conditionally open to visitors.

Marsh Gentian (*Gentiana pneumonanthe*)

The Marsh Gentian, for which Miss Williams had earlier mistaken the Fringed Gentian, is almost as spectacular, with its deep blue trumpets scored on the outside with green lines. As recently as the 1950s, this species was recorded from nearly one in three of the 112 botanical Vice-Counties of Great Britain – with warnings, however, that it had become increasingly local.

It is a plant of damp and acid heaths (not of marshes despite its name) and the development and draining of its habitat are doubtless partly responsible for the decline in its numbers. Suffolk, Essex, Gloucestershire, Somerset and Devon have no recent records. In Norfolk it is scarce. In Sussex it is to be found in suitable habitats on Ashdown Forest and on heathland near Chailey, sometimes in heathy spots favoured by adders. There is also at lest one site by pools in the New Forest along the road from Lyndhurst to Beaulieu Road Station, and plants have been seen there on the very edge of the highway, in late August.

But Dorset is really the plant's headquarters. There it is frequent on the bogs and damp heaths that still remain, and plants with white flowers, both plain and striped with blue, have been recorded. Similar pallid, blue-striped forms occur in a Hampshire site towards the north-east corner of the county. In general, the plants seem to do best where the soil is warm. They are less happy in heathland dominated by large stands of heather, which competes with them for nutrients in the soil.

Mezereon (*Daphne mezereum*)

This enchanting shrub delights the eye in woods as early as mid-February, when its bare twigs are topped with a dip of strawberry-ice-cream-coloured blossom, headed by a single pair of light green leaves. More greenery comes later and, in the places from which the leaves fall in the autumn, new clusters of flowers will decorate the bare wood the following year.

The name Daphne appropriately commemorates the Greek nymph who appealed to the gods to protect her from the attentions of Apollo. They changed her into a laurel bush. Here it is rated as a native plant, probably because it has been found in widely scattered areas, remote from houses, growing where it would grow naturally in continental Europe – mainly on chalk or limestone. North Yorkshire, in particular, has had a number of these remote sites. There are five more remote sites in the Peak District in wooded areas around Lathkilldale and in the valley of the River Manifold. In the chalk downs area which we are discussing in this sector, there has for many years been a well-publicised site within Glynde Holt, a steep escarpment on to the downs north of Glynde village near Lewes.

A score of plants flower in a small wood on the chalk to the north of Henley, some in the clearings growing to their natural height of about 3 feet, others, in rivalry with the privet, to a spindly 6 feet. Unfortunately pheasants are prized more highly there than botanists.

*Monkey Orchid (*Orchis simia*)

It seems that orchid fanciers have taken a particular fancy to this species, perhaps because the loosely disposed 'arms' and 'legs' give a startlingly realistic imitation of a monkey on the end of a stick. Also, the spike of densely packed flowers seems to teem with a vitality lacking in the more stately orchids.

The petals and sepals of the Monkey Orchid are white streaked with pink or violet. They do not form a closed helmet as is the case with the Lady Orchid, the Burnt Orchid and the Military Orchid, but are swept upwards as if to erect a kind of head-dress, leaving the 'face' of the monkey clearly visible. The monkey's 'body' looks long and lithe, the 'arms' seem flexed, and the 'legs' bent as if completing a long-jump. Unusually, the flowers at the head of the spike open first so that, instead of a thin spire of buds at the top, there is a blunt mop of blossom. The whole effect is especially pleasing.

There are only two centres for this plant, both on chalk: the first is on downland high above the Thames, where the orchids are guarded during the flowering season by a warden, and the second on the downs of North Kent. There, the original colony of Monkey Orchids was found at Ospringe, near Faversham, but seed taken from plants there has been sown at other sites by the men of Kent. Try the first week in June.

Musk Orchid (*Herminium monorchis*)

Here is a small green orchid which grows to between 2 and 6 inches, and is thus only slightly taller than that other green orchid, the Bog Orchid. But whereas the latter is found amid well-soaked pads of sphagnum moss, the Musk Orchid grows on dry downland turf where rabbits have kept the coarser grasses at bay.

The upper petals, that is the outer segments of the flowers, grow towards one another, and the lip is held out more or less horizontally, and is pouched beneath – giving the general impression that the flowers are bell-shaped. The lower lip however is sharply pointed, and the inner segments of the flower, which are lance-like, project beyond the rim of the 'bell', thus blurring the image slightly.

The 'English' name is also somewhat confusing, since the flowers, though scented, do not smell of musk.

Though rare and local, this orchid is widely distributed and is regularly reported from the downs of Kent, Surrey, Sussex, Hampshire, Dorset and Wiltshire, as well as from Gloucestershire and parts of the Chilterns. One good locality in West Sussex is on the downs to the south of the small church at Didling, via the A286 road south from Midhurst. A fairly steep climb of perhaps 300 feet up the escarpment of the downs then awaits the visitor. The second week of June is not too early to start looking on this site.

Narrow-leaved Helleborine (*Cephalanthera longifolia*)

This attractive orchid carries a dozen or more white flowers, reminiscent of miniature tulips, on a stem sometimes reaching 2 feet. They are on show in late May in the south of England and perhaps several weeks later on the orchid's northern stations.

In some older works this species appears as the Sword-leaved Helleborine, but the name has been changed, perhaps because the leaves are not invariably flat and swordlike, but are sometimes folded. Their narrowness and length (they sometimes overtop the rest of the plant) are the main features distinguishing this species from its near relative, the White Helleborine (*Cephalanthera damasonium*), which indeed bears leaves that are shorter and broader – and which is, incidentally, far more common and less prodigal with its flowers.

Each flower of the Narrow-leaved Helleborine is decorated with a number of orange ridges on the upper part of the lip, which could serve as nectar guide-lines for the species of small bees which pollinate the flowers.

Despite its rarity, the Narrow-leaved Helleborine is widely scattered. It occurs in the Highlands of Scotland, and in Wales it has been recorded in Monmouthshire, between Chepstow and Tintern, as well as in Cardigan, Merioneth, Caernarvon and Anglesey. There are better sites in Hampshire, including one a mile to the west of East Meon. This is privately owned, managed by the Forestry Commission, and supervised by the Hampshire and Isle of Wight Naturalists' Trust. So ask in advance for a permit.

Pheasant's-eye (*Adonis annua*)

Adonis, the youth beloved of Aphrodite, was killed while on a wild boar hunt, and the blood that he shed gave rise, it was said, to the deep red petals of this plant. Although a native of Greece, Pheasant's-eye was, according to Gerard, well established as a wild plant in England at the end of the sixteenth century.

Like other arable weeds, it has suffered from spraying and the most likely places for it, therefore, are at the edges of the fields where spraying has been less intense or even non-existent. Although it occurs fairly regularly in fields on the chalk to the north-east of Tetbury in Gloucestershire, close to the source of the Thames, Pheasant's-eye is more often seen further south of the river. A favoured area is in Friston Forest near Cuckmere Haven in East Sussex, and in cornfields from Seaford eastwards towards Eastbourne where, at one time, the plants were so common that bunches of the flowers were picked and sent up to Covent Garden market for sale.

In 1978 hundreds of plants appeared at Crowlink in East Sussex, in a field near the sea which had recently been ploughed up. The seeds of *Adonis* had, presumably, either been imported accidentally with other seed or been lying dormant. Anyone seeking to rediscover the plant could do worse than start at Crowlink, in the hope that some plants will have persisted in the area. June onwards.

Red Star-thistle (*Centaurea calcitrapa*)

This is a prickly member of a group which also contains the Cornflower (*Centaurea cyanus*) and the Lesser Knapweed (*Centaurea nigra*), but it is a good deal scarcer, being virtually confined to the chalk downs near the East Sussex coast and to a Kent site above Chatham known as 'The Lines'. It was recorded by Gilbert White in Sussex in 1765, and in Chatham from 1839, and if found elsewhere would probably be a 'casual'. It was presumably introduced in lucerne or clover seed imported from abroad.

It is a striking plant, up to 2 feet tall depending on whether its position is windswept. The branches are 'divaricate', that is they diverge from one another at a wide angle, so that the general impression is of a small bush. Ten or so of the bracts beneath each flower sport an appendage ending in a broad spine up to an inch long giving the plant its starry appearance. The flowers are pinkish-mauve. The flowering season is lengthy – from July to September.

Of the two main sites, that in East Sussex at Cuckmere Haven is the more convenient. It can be reached on either the A26 or the A259. The Information Centre and car-park are on the eastern side of the Exceat Bridge over the Haven River, and a track on the same side of the river leads to the base of the Seven Sisters cliff. The plants, by no means plentiful, are to the left of the track on the way down.

*Rough Marsh mallow (*Althaea hirsuta*)

The coarse and stiff hairs of this plant are but one of the features which distinguish it from the soft and woolly perennial Marsh mallow, *Althaea officinalis*, which in the past was the source of the jellies galore. The 'rough' species is usually an annual, rarely a biennial, and, at 2 feet maximum, stands less than half the height of the true Marsh mallow; unlike its larger cousin, the Rough Marsh mallow prefers disturbed ground on the chalk, particularly round the edges of arable fields. Like the Red Star-thistle, this species may have been introduced from abroad with lucerne or clover seed.

At a site near Aller in the Glastonbury area of Somerset, it persisted from 1875 to 1954; another site a few miles away was discovered in 1950 and has since been watched over by the Somerset Trust for Nature Conservation.

The flowering period is uncertain. Books tend to limit it to a stretch running from mid-July to mid-August, but I have known it in May and in mid-September. The colour of the flowers is variable, too, ranging from delicate pink to pink-lilac and even to mauve.

Kent is the county in which the Rough Mallow is most likely to be on show. Cobham, Cuxton and Strood are traditional sites and, although these localities are 2 to 3 miles apart, the search for this rare plant can be narrowed down to the arable chalk fields within this triangle.

Round-headed Rampion (*Phyteuma orbiculare*)

From a distance this could be a giant blue clover, but the upright, unbranched stem and the long-stalked, occasionally heart-shaped lower leaves are distinctive. The curved florets, massed together in a tousled head, are curved, tubular at first, but later split into five petals.

Gerard, in the 1633 edition of his *Herbal*, wrote that he had received seeds and roots of the plant from Mr Goodyer, 'who found it growing plentifully wilde in the inclosed chalkie hilly grounds by Maple-Durham neere Petersfield in Hampshire'. The following year, 1634, Thomas Johnson, who had edited the new edition of Gerard's *Herbal*, found the plant for himself on the earthwork known as Silbury Hill, 1 mile south of Avebury, on the north side of the by-road between Beckhampton and West Kennett. It has continued to grow there over the centuries.

Formerly widespread in the south, the plant is scarcely known today in Surrey or Kent, but there is a strong colony in Hampshire on Old Winchester Hill (near to West Meon, but by no means adjacent to Winchester). In Sussex, flowers are scattered thinly across the downs, from the Hampshire border eastwards, and a good site exists east of Lewes on the grassy slopes beneath Mount Caborn (grid reference 444-089): the farmer's permission should be sought. Other flowers are to be found on downs to the east of Cuckmere Haven. They appear in July and August but are occasionally on show as early as the first week in June.

Shepherd's Needle (*Scandix pecten-veneris*)

This is a diminutive member of the carrot family, with a lace handkerchief of small white flowers and dainty leaves, divided and sub-divided, sometimes twice, sometimes three times. The fruits of the plant are as coarse as the rest of it is delicate; they are perhaps 2 inches long, including the beaks, pointing upwards like organ pipes. The pipes split apart later to reveal the seeds.

This plant is an annual, and a disappearing one, though it has, at one time or another, been reported from most counties. It is permanently vulnerable since it often grows alongside other weeds which the farmer loves to spray. I make no apology, therefore, for drawing attention again to a site which I discovered myself, where it is unlikely to be sprayed: namely the outer wall of Roedean School on the main coastal road from Brighton to Newhaven. There is a small car-park on a by-road on the west side of, and close to, the school; there is of course no need to enter the school grounds. Indeed the plants often spread on to a grassy bank to the east of the school wall, and are normally on show (there) from April onwards.

Spiked Rampion (*Phyteuma spicatum*)

This rare plant is confined to a relatively limited area of East Sussex bounded by Hadlow Down and Heathfield in the north and Arlington in the south. It is generally regarded as a native plant, although it was not recorded as a living wild plant until 1829 when it was seen on Knight's Farm, Mayfield, a mile from Cross-in-Hand.

The flowers are greenish, or yellowish-white. When in full flower, in June through July, the plants, with unbranched stems rising to a full $2\frac{1}{2}$ feet, can easily be picked out, even in the gloaming of a wood. One traditional site – though they are not as plentiful there as they used to be – is Abbots Wood. This lies a mile to the north of Polegate which is on the A27 between Lewes and Pevensey. The wood is under the supervision of the Forestry Commission and can be entered through a ride which flanks the Forester's Lodge, where the visitor may present himself before starting to explore.

Spiked Rampion is equally happy to grow on the grass verges and banks of the narrow lanes which criss-cross this area, as for instance on Brown's Lane. Similar sites exist among the lanes running south from Hadlow Down. The chances of seeing a clump of plants are, of course, greatly increased if the verges have not yet been cut.

*Starfruit (*Damasonium alisma*)

Starfruit is usually less than a foot high, with leaves which are heart-shaped at the base, 'oblong' or egg-shaped in outline and blunt at the ends.

This water-plant is an on-the-brink annual species in more senses than one since, after having been recorded in some 50 different sites from Hampshire to Essex, Worcester in the west, and Yorkshire to the north, it was confined by 1970 to one site, in Surrey, and for a time failed to appear even there. It had been swamped by mud which had continually drained into its pond. However, after an earth-mover had been used to dredge out some of the autumn mud, a few diminutive specimens reappeared the following year, and some of these have been resited in a protected area nearby.

Starfruit seeds germinate under water in early winter when the water level is high; they will not germinate in mud. In the spring the plant sends up long stalked leaves which float on the surface of the water. But thereafter the plant prospers only in years when the water dries out early in the season leaving the other competing aquatic plants high and dry, so to speak.

Starfruit is in flower from June to August, which means that there is a good chance of seeing both flowers and fruit together. The flowers are white with a yellow spot at the base of the petals. The seeds are carried in carpels which grow from a common centre, gradually spreading out in the shape of a star.

Stinking Hellebore (*Helleborus foetidus*)

Unlike the Green Hellebore (p. 52) the Stinking Hellebore overwinters – that is, its leaves, carried on an almost woody stalk, show above ground throughout the year. The flowers of this plant hang downwards, like pale green, unrinsed wine-glasses, but for some unexplained reason the band of purplish-red wine round the rim of the petals in the wild plants seems to vanish once they enter a garden.

The Hellebore's reputation was made when the Greek shepherd Melampus used it to banish the madness which had afflicted the daughters of Proetus, King of Argos. Equally miraculous powers were attributed to the Stinking Hellebore by our own countrymen when they bestowed on it the name Setterwort. 'Setter' was a corruption of *seta*, the word for the bristle the Romans used when introducing a portion of the Hellebore root into the dewlap – the loose skin beneath the throat – of the animal to be treated. In France, the word became *seton* and referred to a silken thread used for the same purpose. Apothecaries of the Middle Ages called for Hellebore roots to be dug up and used for 'purging downwards flegme, choler, and also melancholy especially', which perhaps helps to explain why the plant has become increasingly rare.

A fine woodland site exists on the north-western slopes of Arundel Park facing towards Amberley. The plant has been recorded in recent years in more than a dozen localities on suitable habitats in the western part of Kent, particularly on either side of the upper reaches of the Medway. Look between March and May.

White Horehound (*Marrubium vulgare*)

This perennial, rather dowdy plant, with dull-green wrinkled leaves and dingy flowers, is unlikely to be 'collected' for the garden, though it may originally have escaped from one.

Plants near our south coast could be native, as they are found consistently in similar habitats, on chalk or on sand near the sea which frequently contains a proportion of lime. However, the White Horehound is much more at home in North Africa, the Canaries and the south of Europe in general than in our undependable climate.

Here, it loves to grow in waste places that can become cultivated, by roadsides which are vulnerable to widening, along hedgerows that are sprayed, and on similar perishable nooks which are more suited to annuals. The *Sussex Plant Atlas* notes that since an earlier survey in 1937 the number of sites in the county for White Horehound has fallen from 50 to seven.

However there is one chalk site in Sussex which could be genuine. This is a stone shed in the neighbourhood of Halnaker Windmill, a landmark visible from the road from Chichester to Petworth, and remote from houses. It is reached by taking the old Roman road, known as Stane Street, starting from a point at grid reference 916-087, and branching left after a few hundred yards on to a farm track leading to the windmill. The shed lies to the right of and slightly below the windmill as you approach it. But the plants might, all the same, originally have come there on the sandals of Roman legionaries. From July on.

White Mullein (*Verbascum lychnitis*)

Seeing this tall pallor of white flowers appearing unexpectedly before one's eyes is almost like meeting a ghost – the spectre perhaps of one of those jolly, yellow mulleins that we botanists have become so used to seeing on the verges of roadsides in July. The sudden loss of colour on a television screen could hardly be more striking than a first meeting with this rare and local plant.

It can be nearly 5 feet tall, with leaves that are dark green above, and powdery white beneath. The flowers appear in July in small groups on the main stem – also densely powdered – and on the branches, white-petalled and surrounded by woolly sepals. The stalks of the stamens also are clothed in white hairs.

North-west Kent is really the headquarters of this species. It flowers on verges and banks along the Pilgrim's Way, that route, probably of prehistoric origin, which runs along the southern slope of the North Downs. But it is also to be found in quarries, and on waste ground, and for that matter in railway yards. There might also be new colonies on the ground disturbed by the construction of the rail links with the Channel Tunnel. In Sussex there are colonies near the northern limits of Arundel Park in places where the scrub has been burnt or cut down. Somerset can boast of a yellow form of this species, which occurs round the villages of Bossington and Selworthy, near Porlock.

3: *New Forest*

Asarabacca (*Asarum europaeum*)

Here is a plant so strange in appearance that the apothecaries of the
Middle Ages could scarcely keep their hands off it. The leaves are of
a salad-bowl green, net-veined and as sweetly rounded as the edge
of a fisherman's net as it is cast over the water. They stand on long
stalks which branch in pairs from close to the rootstock, and then
rise vertically more or less in parallel. Near the base of each pair of
stalks there lurks a single hairy greenish, brownish or purplish
flower, its three petals joined together for most of their length to
form a tube or bell.

As to its nationality there is some doubt. But 'Asarabacca' is a
conjunction of two pre-Christian Greek names chosen by rival
apothecaries for the same plant. They compromised by agreeing to
run both names in tandem.

The experts say that it may be a native plant in a few woods,
mostly in the south and west of the country, but the site known to
most inquisitive botanists is Muddyford Road in the village of
Redlynch in Wiltshire, where it grows on a bank, beneath a hedge
which could once have provided its natural background of hazel
bushes. This is not strictly within the perambulation of the New
Forest, but only a few minutes' drive away. Look for the leaves and
flowers in the first week of April.

Bastard Balm (*Melittis melissophyllum*)

Two-inch flowers, white, pink, or pink-spotted, make this one of the most conspicuous of hedge-bank wild flowers, and, if seen, perhaps one of the most frequently picked. The rococo trumpets, displayed in pairs from the base of the leaf-stalks, match in style the ornate wrinkled and scalloped edges of the dark green leaves. Books tell us that its flowering season is from May to July, but some seekers have been disappointed to find, during the last week of May, that not a petal remained on the plants.

The species is extremely local. There are a number of sites in Cornwall, particularly in the Truro area, and in East Cornwall in the Hawke's Wood Reserve near Wadebridge, managed by the Cornwall Trust for Nature Conservation. The same authority takes care of another open woodland reserve at Luckett, 3 miles north-east of Callington in which the plant has been recorded.

In Devon, the traveller, with luck, may find plants near the Exeter-Barnstaple road, and on hedges and banks in the countryside from Tavistock south-west towards the Cornish border.

Except for a doubtful site at Plummers Plain in mid-Sussex the New Forest may be the most easterly location for the species in Britain. The plants there, limited to two or three, are well away from picnickers in the mid-ride of a large wood. Further details would be at the discretion of the Hampshire and Isle of Wight Naturalists' Trust.

Narrow-leaved Lungwort (*Pulmonaria longifolia*)

This very changeable plant has funnel-shaped flowers which are true blue on some specimens, purple on others and often pink in bud – whence its popular country name, Soldiers and Sailors.

The leaves of the wild species allow us to tell it apart from the garden plant: those arising from the base of the wild plant are eight times are long as broad – even more at the end of their growing season. They are spear-like in outline, and narrow gradually below. Those of the domestic plant are egg-shaped, only one and a half times as long as broad, abruptly narrowing at the base, which is sometimes heart-shaped, and the rounded edges of the leaves contract towards the tip into a sharp point.

This has become a rare plant and, apart from a few sites in the Poole area of Dorset, is confined to Hampshire and the Isle of Wight. One site easily reached by car is on the verge of the road bordering Parkhurst Forest to the north of the prison. On the mainland there is an obliging colony visible from the car. To visit it the motorist should leave Beaulieu by the B3054 going north and take the first main turning to the right for Exbury. After travelling for little more than 2 miles, and crossing a cattle grid, the visitor should keep a sharp eye on the bank to the right of the road. If you reach the entrance to the Exbury Garden Centre you have gone too far.

Late March is the right time.

*Pennyroyal (*Mentha pulegium*)

Once you have seen this Mint, you will never again allow yourself to be put off by near-imitations of it by other commoner species – particularly Corn Mint, which has none of Pennyroyal's pungent sovereign remedy smell. Pennyroyal's special characteristics are a stout, more or less prostrate stem, erect only when flowering; global pincushion whorls of flowers distanced remotely from each other along the main stem; rounded stem-leaves, less than $\frac{3}{8}$ inch broad, looking absurdly small as they poke out from beneath the flowers. There is no terminal flower-head.

This plant leads a threatened existence around the margins of shallow ponds, and depends for its survival on other vegetation in the neighbourhood being soaked away by winter rains or trodden down by animals.

A well-known site – and one of the most easily reached – is in the village of Pilley, approachable from Brockenhurst. Here the edges of the pond are well trodden by ponies and the pond, being shallow, floods and recedes over a comfortably large margin. There is usually plenty of Pennyroyal there, and the plant holds out well even in the driest years when wide cracks appear in the bed of the pond (as it does on another New Forest site managed by the National Trust).

Late August or early September is a suitable time for looking.

*Small Fleabane (*Pulicaria vulgaris*)

This increasingly rare annual herb deserves a mention here, despite its rather commonplace appearance. It produces yellow daisy-flowers not quite half an inch across, each consisting of a central 'plate' or disc, packed with tubular florets, and edged by a rib of yellow rays so short that they remind one of cog-teeth. These disadvantages differentiate the plant from its flashier cousin *Pulicaria dysenterica*, the fully-fledged Fleabane with the longer rays and larger flowers which smiles at the passer-by from every other ditch in southern England towards the end of the summer holidays.

Small Fleabane, like Pennyroyal, discussed above, is found near the edges of ponds or depressions on flat ground, where water stands during the winter and dries out in summer. Under such conditions, few over-wintering plants survive to compete with the Small Fleabane in the spring.

One well-known site – among the best – lies just outside Brockenhurst on the open space known as South Weirs. To reach it, leave the centre of Brockenhurst keeping to the west of the main road leading south from Brockenhurst to Lymington. You will arrive at a small ford – normally carrying only a few inches of water – before reaching open country. Look on the left for a large open space with a track and a row of houses on the east side. That is South Weirs, flat, relatively dry in summer and easily surveyed. Choose the third week in July.

*Wild Gladiolus (*Gladiolus illyricus*)

Inevitably one is surprised to come across such a formal plant, with its bluish-green leaves and deep red flowers, at bay in such a wilderness.

Thirty-eight sites for the Wild Gladiolus are currently known, all of them in the New Forest. But it would probably be unwise to pin-point them. Even in these enlightened days, when a near-equivalent species, *Gladiolus byzanticus*, is stocked by nurserymen, some gardeners prefer to help themselves in the wild. The plant has certainly vanished from 'safe' localities to which visitors were formerly taken in the hope that this would serve to protect the other remaining sites.

Given the open landscape of the New Forest and the number of tourists present, true 'security' becomes especially difficult. Research carried out from 1987 to 1989 by Jonathan Stokes under the supervision of the Nature Conservancy Council and with funds from that body and from the World Wildlife Fund established that, in any one year, a mere 2 per cent of the recorded population developed into mature flowering plants. He found that immature plants were heavily grazed, and that within the layer of stone-free brown earth which alone suits the gladioli there was severe competition from bracken. The plants did better in sectors where the bracken was thinly spaced, or where the light-excluding bracken canopy had been held back by frost damage. But, in places, thick layers of dead bracken hindered the growth of the plants.

The last fortnight in June (before the bracken is fully grown) is the best time to look.

4: *Coastal Area*

*Childing Pink (*Petrorhagia nanteuilii*)

This is a true member of the Pink family, with chaffy bracts like thin manila paper surrounding the flowers, which are less than a centimetre across and of a pale, not very intense pink. The five petals are notched.

There has been some confusion about the vernacular name for this plant, which appears sometimes as Childling as if to imply that this pink is the offspring of some larger mother-pink. Childing, meaning 'child-bearing', would be closer to the adjective *prolifera*, and would, presumably, refer to the apparent ease with which this plant continually produces new flowers, one at a time, from the top of its stem.

In dull weather, or towards evening, the flowers close, and effectively disappear behind their brown paper mantles, leaving only inconspicuous grassy stalks to be seen. This may account for the fact that two groups of experienced botanists surveying its haunts within the same month may come up with widely differing estimates of the number of existing plants.

This is an exceedingly rare species and is now limited to two sites in West Sussex in the area around Pagham Harbour. Its tap-root, growing vertically downwards, allows it to grow on bare shingle in places where few other plants can survive and where bathers, walkers and rabbits seldom tread. It also flourishes on sandy waste ground, along with centaury and other like-minded seaside companions.

The Childing Pink occasionally starts to flower in June.

*Jersey Cudweed (*Gnaphalium luteo-album*)

The white, woolly texture of the leaves and stem, and the straw colour of the bracts surrounding the flower-heads, have earned this species its multi-coloured botanical name. The florets are yellowish, and in the case of the outer, female ones, are decorated with stigmas of a pleasing reddish colour. The height of the erect stem varies according to the growth pattern of the surrounding vegetation. Where the ground surface is bare, the plants may not rise above a few inches, but amid tall herbage they can manage nearly a foot and a half.

Jersey Cudweed is native in the Channel Islands. On the mainland, where it has possibly been introduced, it turns up mainly in coastal areas: on waste ground in Glamorgan, and in Norfolk where its main station is on the dunes between Holkham and Burnham Overy Staithe. In this last area it could well be native, since it grows in similar habitats on the Continent.

Another coastal station is at Holton Heath in the Poole Harbour area, east of the A351 from Lytchet Minster to Wareham. Holton Heath is a Nature Conservancy Council reserve of saltmarsh, reed-bed and heathland, especially noted for its butterfly, spider, reptile and bird populations. Consequently access to the reserve is by permit only. Within the reserve the plants of Jersey Cudweed grow on dumps of ash long ago disinherited by the nearby sewage works.

This is a plant of the late summer, and the flowers should be at their best during the last week of August.

*Late Spider-orchid (*Ophrys holoserica [fuciflora]*)

This flowers later than the Early Spider-orchid (*Ophrys sphegodes*), described here among the rare flowers of the West Country, but not much later: it should be on show within the first ten days of June whereas, in a late year, the 'early' species can still be in flower on 29 May.

In some respects the Late Spider is not unlike the much more common Bee Orchid (*Ophrys apifera*), from which, however, it is easily distinguished by the three-lobed yellow appendage which juts forward from the bottom of its hairy lip. The lip also carries on it circles of canary yellow of a bolder design than that displayed by the Bee Orchid.

There used to be a few plants of the Late Spider-orchid on Sugarloaf Hill, a domed piece of downland wedged between the A20, as it then was, and the A260. Unfortunately, coarse grasses were allowed to take control there, and the orchids disappeared.

The prospects for the survival of this orchid seem to change almost from one month to the next as new plans connected with the Channel Tunnel unfold, but clearly this is a case in which it might be necessary to move some plants, tubers and all, away from lorry parks, railway cuttings, train sidings and the like. *Kent Wildlife Focus*, the colour magazine sent to members of the Kent Trust for Nature Conservation, is a good update on present and future prospects for the survival of this species.

Least Lettuce (*Lactuca saligna*)

Despite its height of up to 3 feet, the Least Lettuce, one of the rarest of British plants, can easily be overlooked. Its branches do not spread, but are held stiffly upright and close to the stem. The stem-leaves are held vertically and usually in a north-south plane, so that in the heat of the day they are edge-on to the sun, and so less prone to lose their precious moisture. The flowers close when the weather is unpropitious.

There are colonies along the Thames estuary mainly in the shelter of the sea walls where cattle roam, creating areas of bare ground where the Least Lettuce, being an annual, can spring up and prosper without interference from other vegetation. It also needs warm weather in the spring months if it is to flower, as it normally does, during July and August.

The Kent areas for the plant are around Cliffe marshes, some 5 miles north of Rochester, and at Seasalter, to the west of Whitstable. In Essex the best-known site is at Fobbing, about 4 miles south of Basildon. Least Lettuce has also survived amid the shingle and sand of Rye Harbour. There is sometimes a small patch to be seen in the Rye Harbour Nature Reserve on the bank to the east side of the road, opposite the first of the hides built for birdwatchers, though this is not the only site on the reserve, and inevitably locations vary from year to year.

*Lizard Orchid (*Himantoglossum hircinum*)

As many as 80 flowers can be seen on a single plant of the
unmistakable Lizard Orchid. Gerard called it a bush – it can be 3 feet
high – and drew attention to the 'writhen' (twisted as in a wreath)
tails and spotted heads of the flowers which suggested lizards to the
average observer. The petals forming the lizard's 'head' remain
permanently joined together in a skull-like shape.

In the 1920s and '30s this species seemed to be on the increase in
Britain, and findings were reported from Norfolk, Suffolk, on the
Devil's Dyke in Cambridgeshire and at Hinxton in the same county
where, unfortunately, it perished in a tramp's bonfire. There were
finds in Oxfordshire and, sporadically, in Somerset. In Sussex, it
appeared on Goodwood racecourse, and for some years there has
been a dwindling colony near the Kent border. Kent, where it has
been known since 1641, seems to be its true home and as recently
as the 1980s it could be seen close to the roadside on the beach at
Sandwich. The verdict seems to be that this species is on the
decrease at the moment, but that the seeds can lie dormant and
germinate after many seasons. It favours chalk, including calcareous
dunes, and is partial to a breath of sea air. Just across the Channel,
it is a common wayside plant. Try late June or early July.

Mouse-tail (*Myosurus minimus*)

The name refers to the tapering spike of closely packed fruits which ripen above each of the greenish-yellow flowers of this rare member of the buttercup family. Four inches would be an average height for the plant. The flowering season varies between April and July according to the latitude and the weather.

In general, this is a lowland plant, and is less scarce in the south and east of the country than in the north. Like the Least Lettuce, the Mouse-tail prefers bare waste ground, especially those areas that have been well trodden by cattle and which, in consequence, have held water during the winter. One of the best sites in the Isle of Wight is close to a gateway used by horses, and a small pond nearby at which they drink. The dampest corner of any damp field is a possible hiding place if the ground is sufficiently bare.

It seems likely, too, that the plant is not averse to a little sea air. This is particularly the case in Essex, where more than half the sites for Mouse-tail are close to, or actually on, the sea walls. The number of plants increased considerably after the great flood of 1953 and the disturbance of the ground which followed during the reconstruction of the sea defences. The best locations are in the area south and east of Colchester down as far as St Osyth.

In West Sussex Mouse-tail persists at Pagham on the edge of a field adjoining the caravan site at grid reference 879-970, close to a drain through which water periodically floods.

Sand Catchfly (*Silene conica*)

The flowers, set like pink Catherine wheels, are pygmy-sized: barely half as big as those of the Small-flowered Catchfly. Yet the Sand Catchfly, with its stiffly erect stem topped by striped, swollen, conical calyces, remains one of the most interesting and unusual members of the Pink 'family'. It is also one of the rarest, having apparently disappeared from many former sites, as for instance from Sussex at Shoreham, and from Kent. In East Anglia, we are told in *The Flora of Norfolk*, it is 'much rarer than formerly'.

It is an annual species and appears in varying numbers and slightly different places from one season to the next. In England it is a native plant, but in Wales it is looked on as a 'naturalised alien (England)'. It has been recorded in Scotland from Montrose and from the golf links of Arbroath, before the dunes there were levelled. Golf courses, where there is a dry climate, good drainage, short grass and sand with some calcium content, seem to be the favoured habitat, particularly where the ground or the vegetation has been disturbed.

One location, known for at least a century, is near the mouth of the River Arun in Sussex, where it grows along the coast to the west for nearly half a mile towards Clymping. Plants can often be viewed from outside Littlehampton golf course through the barbed wire perimeter fencing.

Mid-June is probably the safest time.

Sea Pea (*Lathyrus japonicus, subspecies maritimus*)

This is a very special feature of the Rye Harbour Nature Reserve in East Sussex, and freely exposed there, for the plants are to be seen on either side of the reserve's main road where it turns to run parallel with the sea-shore.

The blue-green, almost egg-shaped leaflets contrast agreeably with the rosy-purple (or purplish-rose if this description is preferred) standards and whitish keels of the flowers. The pods have a markedly swollen appearance and have, at a pinch, in bygone times served as food. The seeds are able to germinate after having been soaked in sea-water for as long as four or five years. Yet in Britain the Sea Pea is by no means common, for a place by the sea is not usually acceptable to it unless the site contains solid shingle and is clear above the high-tide mark.

These requirements are fully met in parts of Suffolk between Felixstowe and Lowestoft, especially where shingle has built up against newly erected groins. But trampling by visitors and bulldozing by developers have reduced the numbers in some areas, particularly to the south of Aldeburgh. There are a brace of colonies on the east coast of Essex, and a smattering of sites on the east coast of Kent where shingle occurs from Dungeness northwards to Deal. In Dorset, as might have been expected, it is found on Chesil Beach between Chickerell and Portland in the east and at Abbotsbury in the west. Flowers June to August.

*Small Hare's-ear (*Bupleurum baldense*)

'Small' is certainly the right adjective for the plants to be seen on mainland Britain, and the minute yellow flowers shown on this photograph are at least twice life-size. The two large brown 'wings' pointing respectively to the left and right of the flowers are bracts, and the smaller, greener, pointing 'shields' in the background are bracteoles, which are said in some works to conceal the flowers and fruits, though not, fortunately in this instance.

It is hard to believe that this little plant, less than 2 inches tall, is a member of the family which includes the lordly Caraways, Fennel and other similar species with stalks growing out together from the top of the main stem, like spokes from an umbrella. In this case, it would appear that there are only two such rays, each with its group of small, almost stalkless yellow flowers, with petals in-turned at the tips.

There are only two locations for this rare plant on the mainland, the first on Berry Head, on the southern margin of Tor Bay. This nature reserve is in the care of Torquay Borough Council which provides a leaflet describing several other rare plants to be found on this unique site. The alternative and more accessible site (for Londoners) is on the downland turf to the west of the Beachy Head lighthouse for which the approximate grid reference is 576-953. Here the plants delight to grow as near as possible to the edge of the cliff – especially where it has begun to crumble – in positions varying from year to year. The beginning of June is the right time.

Starry Clover (*Trifolium stellatum*)

The species is so called because the teeth of the calyx, which are clothed with dense white hairs, suggest unlit stars, waiting to explode into brilliance. The minute flowers are bunched together in dense globe-shaped heads, which are white at their best but flecked later with pink as the flowers begin to die off. The trefoil leaves are blunt and nicked at the end.

This species is now a rarity confined to a single area of West Sussex. It is believed to have entered there in 1809 in the ballast of ships returning from Wellington's Peninsular campaigns. But somehow it has hung on, reappearing here and there, sometimes quite unexpectedly, for it is an annual.

The plant appears more often on waste ground in New Shoreham than in Old Shoreham. One site on which Starry Clover could reappear is on waste ground along Riverside Road where it once almost completely covered the unmown lawn of a private garden. There are a number of other propitious sites on cleared ground close to the sea front, including one provided with a bench against which the plant has been known to nestle. Late May is the right time to be looking.

5: *Isle of Wight*

*Field Cow-wheat (*Melampyrum arvense*)

The purple bracts give this plant an unusually 'sharp' look. Its tubular flowers seem somewhat bizarre too: open-mouthed, with purple blotches on lips and throat and a large orange disc on each side. The height is up to 18 inches. Cow-wheat seeds were known to discolour the flour and were difficult to separate from the wheat, so many farmers took steps to uproot plants and burn them. Stubble-burning and the removal of hedges and ditches has probably killed off many plants. Today, with stricter controls on imported seed, the chances of a revival in the numbers of Field Cow-wheat plants seem slim.

Only a handful of sites remain. Essex claims one traditional locality at Bartholomew Green, 3 miles south-west of Braintree, where varying numbers of plants have grown over the years in a cornfield hedge and nearby ditch. Some plants grow in Bedfordshire in the grass around excavations, but while they are not in danger from the farmer's spray they could well be swamped by the exuberance of the surrounding vegetation.

Two more sites still exist in the extreme south-east of the Isle of Wight, where one colony flourishes on a steep bank or near-cliff overlooking a group of houses. The second site is in the long grass of one corner of a hill-top field. Here again there is little possibility of intrusion by the plough. Both sites are tended by volunteers from the Hampshire and Isle of Wight Naturalists' Trust. Late summer.

126

Hoary Stock (*Matthiola incana*)

It is the leaves that are hoary, of course, and not the flowers. The main stem or 'stock' of this plant is woody and leafless, but it gives rise to a number of branches on which the leaves, narrow, pointed and entire, persist in rosettes into the following year. The flowers, like those of other members of the cabbage family, are four-petalled and normally, though not invariably, deep purple, of a shade well set off by the frosty greenery around them.

Some British botanists would have liked to claim this as a native plant, but the French *savants* declare that it is truly native only in the southern part of their country, and that in the north of France it is an introduced plant. Nevertheless in Britain it has been well established in the wild, and accepted as such for more than a century in at least three localities.

One of these is above the Brighton Marina at the eastern end of the town, where the stocks grow between the main road and the sea on the very edge of the cliff, and in some places some way down it.

On the Isle of Wight the principal site for Hoary Stock is at Afton Down on the south-west coast of the island, on the edge of the cliffs, on National Trust property. A second site is on the south coast of the island, between Ventnor and St Lawrence, where, however, white and pink flowers are on show as well as purple.

Yarrow Broomrape (*Orobanche purpurea*)

Yarrow Broomrape is distinguished by its colour and by the three bracts which surround each flower. It is a parasitic plant which attaches underground tubers to the roots of the host plant. One could be excused, therefore, for thinking that the host-plant – in this case Yarrow – was being 'raped' by the attendant parasite. But, as Geoffrey Grigson reminded us in his classic work, *The Englishman's Flora*, the name was suggested by a feature of the first generally known Broomrape, *Orobanche rapum-genistae*, the Greater Broomrape, which is parasitic on Broom. And the tuber of the Greater Broomrape is globe-shaped, and thus similar to the root of the Turnip, otherwise known as Rape: hence Broomrape.

On the Isle of Wight, however, it has been recorded from at least three sites around Sandown, Shanklin and Newchurch, 2 miles north-west of Sandown. It is seen most consistently on the Red Cliff, near Culver, to the north-east of Sandown. A glance from the beach before starting to climb shows that the cliff is sharply divided into two sectors, the nearer being made up of red sandy soil while the other consists of chalk. The boundary between these two sectors offers the best prospects for success, and the second week of June is normally the best time to look for the Yarrow Broomrape. By then, there should be plenty of Yarrow leaves to act as markers, even though no Yarrow flowers would yet be showing.

AREA TWO: THE WEST COUNTRY

*Cheddar Pink (*Dianthus gratianopolitanus*)

The Cheddar Gorge – or, to be more accurate, the carboniferous
limestone cliffs above it – is the only site for this species west of the
Belgian Ardennes. It was found there, at least by 1724, by a Mr
Samuel Brewer, a woollen manufacturer of Trowbridge, who sought
solace in botany when past the age of 50, after his business had
failed and he had quarrelled with his family.

The Cheddar Pink grows in dense tufts, with many long,
procumbent, non-flowering bluish-green shoots. The flowers are
carried, usually singly, on upright stalks about 8 inches tall. The
flowers average 1 inch across – larger than those of any other of our
wild pinks – and vary in colour from deep pink to pale rose. They
are deeply scented. The petals are fretted with short, irregular teeth.

The public first became interested in the Cheddar Pink after the
road had been cut in 1801 to open up the Gorge. At that time whole
sectors of the rocks were still rose-tinted with drifts of pinks, and for
years afterwards seeds cast from above led to Cheddar Pinks growing
by the roadside. That is no longer the case today; over the years, the
wishes of those gardeners who were unwilling to climb the cliffs
were gratified by the villagers, who retailed plants they had
themselves uprooted. Nowadays a visit to the Cheddar Pink involves
a substantial climb on to more or less open downland above the
cliffs, and perhaps the use of binoculars. June and early July are best.

(Cornish) Bladderseed (*Physospermum cornubiense*)

It seems strange that this species which, outside Britain, grows only south of the Alps in countries such as Portugal, Spain, the Balkans, Cyprus and Syria, should be able to weather our own climate. But it does so in a score of locations in East Cornwall where, one suspects, it must be a relic from long, long ago when Britain and Ireland were linked across a land-bridge to Spain and North Africa. The seeds – or, rather, the fruits – when fully developed are broader than long and have an inflated appearance, looking fit to burst. They are the colour of oak-apples.

One of the better-known localities is in Silver Valley almost adjoining the main A390 road from Callington to Gunnislake. The valley is on the south side of the road, starting from grid reference 381-705. An equally rewarding site is reached from Luckett, a village bordering the River Tamar, on a grid reference of 389-737. Park the car in the village, follow the footpath southwards along the river-bank, enter the reserve on the right and follow uphill on to the open ground above, where there are scores of plants.

Other excellent sites are in the neighbourhood of Clapper Bridge some 3 miles south of Callington on grid reference 352-653. Plants have also been recorded on New Down, on the left-hand side of the road from Callington to Clapper Bridge.

Look in July and August.

Dorset Heath (*Erica ciliaris*)

The flowers of Dorset Heath have been described as urceolate, that is pitcher-shaped, in other words sharply constricted at the mouth. In profile, they are curved above and 'inflated' beneath. The style or column connecting the ovary to the stigma on which the pollen is collected projects from the mouth. The flowers are often carried on one side only of the stem. They appear in July.

Their colour is also distinctive, having an element of brick-red in it. In contrast the flowers of Bell Heather (*Erica cinerea*) look purpler, and those of Cross-leaved Heath (*Erica tetralix*) are paler pink. The leaves are arranged around the stems in whorls of three.

In Cornwall, most of the colonies lie in the western part of the county, within a diamond-shaped area between Truro on the south coast, Redruth to the west of Truro, Perranporth on the north coast, and Mitchell to the east of Perranporth. In Dorset, the most accessible site is on the Arne peninsula to the east of Wareham. To reach it, take the A351 road south from Wareham, turn left at Stoborough and continue straight on for nearly 4 miles until the road forks to the right, with a linkage between the two branches. Colonies of Dorset Heath are to be found within and around the resulting small triangular enclosure. There are many other sites among the heathers of the Arne peninsula, and Hartland Moor.

*Early Spider-orchid (*Ophrys sphegodes*)

With its pale greenish flower-segments, and sober brown velvet lip, the Early Spider-orchid cannot hope to rival the more startling colour display of its cousin, the much commoner Bee Orchid; yet somehow it looks far more suited to its surroundings. Four inches is quite a normal height for this species, at least at the start of its flowering season. The lip of the Early Spider-orchid is marked with a device which has been compared to a capital H. When the flowers are still at their best, the H retains a bluish metallic lustre, which gradually fades to silver as the flowers age.

Today the orchid is reported only from Kent, Sussex, Hampshire and Dorset. In Kent there are scattered plants on the downs both north and south of Dover, and there is a strong colony in the Queendown Warren Reserve, south from Hartlip across the M2 motorway. In Sussex there are scattered plants on the chalk around Beachy Head, and there is also a strong colony on the downs further west.

Dorset, however, is the home county for this species, and the fact that the Early Spider-orchid grows on the limestone cliff-tops on the Isle of Purbeck is sufficiently well known to have merited inclusion in *The Macmillan Guide to Britain's Nature Reserves*. Indeed anyone taking the public footpath along the Dorset coast westward from Durlston Head near Swanage has a good chance of seeing an Early Spider-orchid without leaving the footpath, in early May.

*Field Eryngo (*Eryngium campestre*)

For all its prickles, the Field Eryngo is not a member of the Thistle family, but rather of the Cow Parsley tribe. It is taller (up to 2 feet), more spindly in habit, and withal more pallid than its blue-green cousin the Sea Holly (*Eryngium maritimum*) and, whereas the latter has egg-shaped heads of sky-blue flowers closely surrounded by spiny bracts, Field Eryngo has clover-like heads of white flowers standing free from the very long, narrow, pale green bracts beneath and around them.

In the late seventeenth century, in John Ray's time, it was known as Common Eryngo, and he was sent a specimen by a Mr Thornton 'who had observed it not far from Daventry in Northamptonshire, beside the old Roman Way, called Watling-street, near a village called Brookhall' (which is why the plant was at one time known as the Watling-street Thistle). Ray himself met it 'on a rock which you descend to the Ferry from Plymouth over into Cornwall'.

Today Ray's site, or at least the area round it, is the only dependable rendezvous for this plant, and there is, it would seem, an admirable principle of *laissez-faire* which allows it to flourish on the municipal flower-beds. The ones to look at are in the Stonehouse area, not immediately adjacent to the ferry but further south on Western King Point with a view over towards Drake's Island. Late July is the right time to take a stroll round this sector.

Field Garlic (*Allium oleraceum*)

The adjective *oleraceus*, we are told by Professor William T. Stearn in his standard work *Botanical Latin*, means 'pertaining to kitchen gardens either as a pot-herb or vegetable, or as a weed'. This may have been the case when Linnaeus was doling out the names two centuries ago. Since then, however, the Field Garlic has been ousted from the vegetable patch by other more aggressive Garlics.

We are left with a native wild plant of unassuming appearance, and bell-like flowers of no very decisive colour – some say 'pinkish', others 'greenish' and others again 'brownish'. The spathes, or papery shields which initially protect the inflorescence, are unusually long; and as the photograph shows, one of them has outstripped the whole plant. The stamens do not project beyond the petals of the flowers, a distinction which differentiates the Field Garlic from some other Garlic species.

This is a local plant which is to be looked for on waste ground – sometimes on the edges of fields – especially in eastern counties where the soil is dry. There is, however, one dependable site, in the area known as Durdham Down above the Avon Gorge near Bristol. Here the soil is somewhat arid, the grass is thin, and the plants are present in abundance.

This photograph was taken on 3 August during an exceptionally dry summer, so perhaps in a normal season it might be unwise to expect to see the flowers much earlier, whatever the books say.

Goldilocks Aster (*Aster linosyris*)

The individual daisy-flowers have no rays, but *en masse* at the tops of the stems they present radiant, gently swaying aureoles of gold to justify their popular nickname. Dozens of narrow, unstalked, overlapping leaves encompass the stem like fine seaweed across a breakwater. A picturesque plant but a rare one: indeed there are probably no more than seven sites in the whole of Britain for this plant.

All are in the west of the country. Lancashire has the most northerly site – on Humphrey Head, which juts out into the sea from the northern rim of Morecambe Bay. It is steep and not easily accessible. Next there is the Great Orme's Head, another limestone headland staring out to sea. Other seaward sites are at Castlemartin, Pembrokeshire, the Gower Peninsula to the west of Swansea, and Berry Head in south Devon. One of the more accessible localities is in north Somerset near the village of Uphill a few miles south of Weston-super-Mare. The site is best approached along a track which starts from a grid reference of 316-585 and leads south past a disused quarry. The flowers can be seen from the track, on a gentle hill to the left of the farm gate across the track. The map reference for the site is approximately 317-582. Do not try too early for this plant. The third week of September is about right.

Hairy Greenweed (*Genista pilosa*)

This plant, the rarest of the brooms, is a small shrub with stout stems twisted and much branched, grey in their first youth and brown when older.

It can be distinguished from its much commoner look-alike Petty Whin (*Genista anglica*), because the latter is armed with spines. Hairy Greenweed has none. Its other close relative, Dyer's Greenweed (*Genista tinctoria*), is hairy only along the leaf margins, whereas in the case of *G. pilosa* the undersides of the leaves are whitened with closely pressed hairs, and there are fine hairs even on the petals of the flowers.

This is a heathland plant, and has suffered both from heath fires and from reclamation for farming. In Suffolk it has not been seen since 1965; in Kent not this century; in East Sussex it has repeatedly been reported as extinct and then refound again in Ashdown Forest (East Sussex).

There are a handful of sites in Pembrokeshire, particularly around the small sandy cove of Porthmynawyd, which can be reached by walking from the A487 to the Coast Path around St Bride's Bay.

There are other stations, still further west, around St David's Head, and, in Cornwall, it can be found in several spots along the coastal path from Mullion south to Caerthillian and on the north coast between St Agnes and Perranporth. Flowers are to be looked for in May and June – about the same time as those of the Common Broom.

Heath Lobelia (*Lobelia urens*)

This is a rare purple-flowered plant of the late summer, which does best on damp acid heathland. In the early 1980s when the *British Red Data Book for Vascular Plants* was published, there were only ten remaining sites and there has been some concern over the future prospects for this species. It sometimes has a tendency to discontinue flowering on sites subjected to benign neglect. At an East Sussex location, very close to the Kent border, the number of flowering plants increases dramatically after the damp woodland in which it grows has been coppiced, and then declines until the next coppicing takes place. Similarly the number of flowering plants on a privately owned site just beyond the south-west border of the New Forest could well increase if the scrub and bracken were cleared.

The largest colony of Heath Lobelia in Britain is in the reserve to the north of Kingsbridge, owned, since 1986, by the Devon Trust for Nature Conservation. The site covers 58 acres (23 hectares) of wet woodlands and heathy grassland which has not been farmed since 1904. However, it can be reached only by crossing other private farmland under arrangements made by the Trust on behalf of its members. A more readily accessible site is on the north side of the road from Lostwithiel (Cornwall) to Lerryn in the marshy heath behind Redlake Cottage on grid reference approximately 127-588.

Hutchinsia (*Hornungia petraea*)

This is one of the smallest of the crucifer (cross-bearing) family – a little gem, barely 3 inches high, with greenish-white petals. The dark green leaflets are set in pairs on either side of a central leaf-stalk – an arrangement described as pinnate or more accurately pinnatisect since each leaflet is cut short at the base into an elliptical segment.

The basal leaves are arranged in a rosette formed during the November rains, after which the plant remains apparently dormant. Towards the end of February, if the weather be favourable, it springs to life, and within a fortnight can bear flowers and fruit. Branches are formed which continue to grow during the flowering season and while the fruits, each on separate stalks, ripen. By the time the dry months of summer follow, the plants are safely in seed.

Hutchinsia is an annual, but succeeds in establishing itself, year after year, within a few feet of its chosen site. This is most often on limestone rocks or sand-dunes formed partly of sea-shells rich in chalk. One well-known site is in the Avon Gorge on the rocks immediately below Durdham Down and on rocks close to footpaths in the woods below. There are sites in the Gower, beneath Pennard Castle, on limestone rocks in Brecon, Pembrokeshire and Caernarvon, and on ledges in the limestone areas of the Peak District.

The vernacular name was bestowed in honour of an Irish botanist, Miss Ellen Hutchins of Ballylickey, Co. Cork.

Irish Spurge (*Euphorbia hyberna*)

Telling one species of Spurge from another often involves the use of a lens to examine in detail the flower and, later, the fruit. But in the case of the Irish Spurge, the general 'look' of the 2-foot-high plant may suffice. The leaves, in particular, are unusually oblong, rounded at the base, and come close to half-clasping the stem. The bracts beneath the flowers are bright yellow, especially when the sun is on them. In the case of the Wood Spurge (*Euphorbia amygdaloides*), to which Irish Spurge has a superficial resemblance, the leaves are pointed, and tend to be crowded together towards the top of the stem; and the bracts beneath the flowers are joined together, at least partially, to form a cup.

The flowers of Irish Spurge are at their best from May to July, later than those of the Wood Spurge which show from April to June.

Irish Spurge is locally common in woods and banks in the south of Ireland from Kerry to Waterford, in Limerick and, to a lesser degree, in Galway, Mayo, Clare and Donegal. On the mainland of Britain, where it is regarded as a native species, it seems to have disappeared from its former station in Somerset, but is clinging on in West Cornwall, near Portreath. In North Devon, however, the moist and shady area south-east of Lynton seems to suit the plant perfectly. There are stands of it close to Watersmeet, and above it by the lanes between Hillsford and Rockford, where it can be seen even on south-facing verges.

Large-flowered Butterwort (*Pinguicula grandiflora*)

This plant is native in the Republic of Ireland, but not so in the UK. At least three attempts to naturalise it have been made in Cornwall, the best known of which was at Tremethick Cross, about 3 miles west of Penzance. None succeeded, but the men of Somerset have met with greater good fortune, and a thriving colony has been established in Lorna Doone country near the south bank of the Oare stream close to Robbers' Bridge.

Park the car at the bridge, walk over to the south bank of the stream and follow the footpath eastwards for perhaps a mile, until reaching the flush on which the plants grow. Water flows over these rocks even during the driest summer.

An equally watery site has been chosen with success for the Large-flowered Butterwort in Derbyshire, near the start of the Pennine Way in the Vale of Edale, to the east of Chapel-en-le-Frith. Starting from the village of Edale, walk up the Pennine Way, following the stream known locally as Grindsbrook for about a mile, looking to the left for the prominent rock-face decorated by the plants.

The flowers of *Pinguicula grandiflora* are up to $\frac{3}{4}$ inch wide, nearly twice the size of those of the Common Butterwort (P. vulgaris), and the petals are crumpled, with the lobes of the lower lip growing close together or even overlapping. The petals of the Common Butterwort, on the other hand, are flat and not crumpled, and the outer lobes of the lower lip grow out to the side and away from the middle lobe. May to June is the flowering season.

Long-headed Clover (*Trifolium incarnatum subsp. molinerii*)

This extremely rare plant, found only on the Lizard peninsula and in Jersey, is now regarded as a joint sub-species on an equal footing with Crimson Clover, an alien from the Mediterranean formerly grown as a forage plant and now naturalised in southern counties. Long-headed Clover, however, has cream-coloured, not crimson, flowers and, whereas Crimson Clover grows to a foot or more and is erect, Long-headed Clover is usually less than 8 inches high and is semi-recumbent. It is distinguished from other cream-coloured clovers by its densely hairy calyx, but its general appearance and situation ensure that it is not easily confounded.

On the Lizard peninsula it loves to grow amid short grass in places reached by the sea spray. It is an annual and therefore moves from place to place each year. For those with little time to spare, the place to look for it is in the Lizard village itself. Walk to the seaward end of the village and look for the beginning of the coastal path leading northwards towards Mullion. There, up against the wooden skirting to the coastal path on the seaward side, more or less opposite a stall selling ice-cream cornets, there has for some years been a colony of a dozen or so plants, in a nook which offers them both sunshine and spray. However, it is rather more satisfying to discover Long-headed Clover further along the coastal path, first among the low hills close to the sea, and later on the barer uplands in early June.

*Plymouth Pear (*Pyrus cordata*)

This has been described as a tall Crab-like (i.e. Crab-apple-like) shrub but the size varies according to the surroundings. When flanked by tall trees it can reach 30 feet; but in a hedgerow its proportions are more modest. Given enough space, it produces suckers which display some, at least, of its distinguishing features – in particular the armament of sharp thorns which are not invariably a characteristic of the ordinary wild Pear, *Pyrus communis*. Some, but not all, of the leaves are cordate.

There are other differences between the two species in the flowers and fruit, which, in the case of the Plymouth Pear, are not pear-shaped but obovate, that is, similar in shape to an egg left standing on its point. The flowers are smaller, more widely scattered and less bunched together than those of the common Pear. Also, the sepals fall away from the top of the fruit, and do not persist as is the case with *P. communis*.

The Plymouth Pear has been growing in hedges around Plymouth – and, it was believed, nowhere else – for at least a century, though it is less common there than formerly. Many pilgrims, nevertheless, have been to inspect it on hedges around the Estover Industrial Estate, a mile south-east of Plymouth's airport. More recently, at least two new trees have come to light in the lanes less than 2 miles south-west of Truro, thus breaking Plymouth's century-old monopoly. Mid-May is usually the latest date for seeing the blossom and incipient fruits.

Pyrenean Lily (*Lilium pyrenaicum*)

There can hardly be a more beautiful wild flower than this stately lily, with its wax-like petals of greenish lemon-yellow turned back and adorned with dotted guide-lines of the deepest red, plus anthers that suggest ingots of red-hot metal. The leaves, unstalked and upward-pointing, are disposed in two ranks in alternating positions and form a close-knitted green ruff as distinctive as the flowers themselves.

This plant was already popular in English gardens by the end of the sixteenth century, according to John Gerard who knew it as 'the yellow mountaine Lilly with the spotted floure', and drew attention to its Pyrenean origin.

No doubt some of the Pyrenean Lilies growing in the wild were carried there in a garden wheelbarrow. But others established themselves in different ways using other methods of transport. One Scottish site, on a by-road west of Kirriemuir, with an approximate grid reference of 359-532, is remote from gardens, and the much better known site between South Molton and Bampton in Devonshire, with an approximate grid reference of 789-275, is equally isolated. This last site, known to locals for at least 60 years, is on the top of a steep, high, south-facing bank with extensive views to the south, which suggests that the seeds of this lily, which are winged, might have been carried there by the prevailing winds. Flowers on the top of the bank should be out by the third week in May, those lower down a little later.

*Red Helleborine (*Cephalanthera rubra*)

The flowers of this all-too-attractive orchid are of an intense rose-pink which differentiates it entirely from its near-relative, the Dark Red Helleborine (*Epipactis atrorubens*), with its brick-red inflorescence.

The three most frequently mentioned current sites for the Red Helleborine are in the Workman Reserve (care of the Gloucester Naturalists' Society), a long-known site in Buckinghamshire, and a location discovered one Sunday morning in 1986 in a privately owned beech and yew wood in Hampshire. Research into the life-style of this species shows, however, that there may be a dozen more further potential sites. In the first place, the orchid, supplied with food by fungi, is capable of leading a totally subterranean life for years at a stretch and of storing enough food underground in its roots to enable it to send up leaves whenever conditions above ground are propitious. For the orchid, conditions improve when the tall tree canopy is cut away to allow more light. Secondly, only a small proportion of the emergent plants flower, so many could have been overlooked. Thus preparation and investigation of the sites of the past could lead to new finds. There are several such former sites in Gloucestershire alone as, for instance, at the Cooper's Hill Nature Reserve south-east of Gloucester on grid reference 886-142, in nearby Cranham Wood on grid reference 910-130, and at Wootton-under-Edge. Try the first half of July.

Rosy Garlic (*Allium roseum*)

There are two types – sub-species – of Rosy Garlic, namely those
that invariably produce bulbils among their flowers, and those that
invariably don't. Those with bulbils are the kind more often seen,
though by no means frequently. Two noted botanists, David
McClintock and R.S.R. Fitter, give this species their highest rarity
rating; one standard work describes it as 'naturalised in several
places' and another, with greater caution, as 'naturalised in a
number of places'.

At their best, the bell-shaped flowers, bunched together in a head,
despite their long stalks, emit a truly roseate glow. The botanist in
mid-Sussex can see a show of them together with another rarity, the
Few-flowered Garlic (*Allium paradoxum*), on the eastern verge of the
A2037 leading south from the village of Henfield. But both plants
are thought to have escaped from the nearby garden of William
Borrer, the nineteenth-century botanist.

A rather large colony can be seen on the cliffs near St Vincent's
Rock above the Avon Gorge. Unfortunately, however, they have
grown, or been planted, on terrain which might or might not bear
the weight of a man, and no close acquaintance is feasible. A better,
if more remote, site occurs in Cornwall, on the right-hand side of the
lane leading to the National Trust car-park above Kynance Cove.
Rosy Garlic is frequent too in the Isles of Scilly. June is a good time
to be there.

*Sand Crocus (*Romulea columnae*)

Although this diminutive member of the Iris family is barely an inch in stature, its star-shaped flowers can be nearly $\frac{1}{2}$ inch across. Outside, they are white with a touch of green, and inside there is gold at the base of the flowers and purplish guide-lines. The plant has been well known since 1726 on the cliff-tops and dunes of the Channel Islands (though not in gardens even for the most green-fingered plantsmen, which is one reason for regarding it as a native wild plant).

On the mainland there is one site only: on the south coast of Devon at Dawlish Warren, known locally as the Inner Warren. This is a local nature reserve, owned partly by the Devon Trust for Nature Conservation and partly by Teignbridge District Council. Some sections of the reserve, however, including the short turf on which the plants particularly flourish, form part of the Warren Golf Club, which is owned by the Trust but leased to the Golf Club, and there is no access to the course even for Trust members unless, presumably, they can first gain permission from the Club Secretary.

The flowers open fully only when the sun shines, and on dull days, when the petals are closed and only the greenish outsides are visible, it is hard to distinguish the Sand Crocus from the surrounding grass, especially as the leaves themselves are wiry and grass-like.

This plant is an early developer, and the first half of April is not too early for a visit.

Sea Stock (*Matthiola sinuata*)

This Stock has no prescriptive right to be called Sea Stock, since Hoary Stock is often drenched with salt spray and seems to thrive on it. However *sinuata*, meaning 'strongly waved', is acceptable in relation to the lower leaves of Sea Stock, although sometimes they are deeply lobed almost to the mid-rib. The leaves are marked with black dots, the outward and visible sign of the profusion of glands with which the plant is clothed. The pale mauve flowers are small and lack the brilliance of the petals of the Hoary Stock but the rarity and decreasing numbers of Sea Stock make the plant a prize. And it is a truly native species.

Today there are probably no more than four areas in the whole of the British Isles where Sea Stock is to be found: Devon, Glamorgan, Pembrokeshire and the Channel Islands.

The Devon site on Saunton Cliffs, mentioned by R.S.R. Fitter in his invaluable work *Finding Wild Flowers*, is probably the best known and the most easily approached, for the cliffs are little more than sand-dunes. A second site has more recently come to light in mid-Glamorgan on the seaward side of the Kenfig Nature Reserve near Bridgend, and it is possible that the seed may have come from a third reserve near Swansea. In such cases the dunes are the most propitious sites and the plant's stature of 2 feet or so makes it fairly conspicuous. The flowering season is long – mid-May to mid-July.

Spiked Star-of-Bethlehem (*Ornithogalum pyrenaicum*)

Despite its ornate, almost rococo good looks, the 'Spike fashioned Star-floure' as it was formerly called is a genuine native species, known for centuries to have grown wild in Britain. The flowers are greenish-white and, alas, are not always at their best at the same time on individual spikes. At a height of 2 feet, the flowers at the tops of the spikes tower above the surrounding grass and can often be glimpsed from a (slow-) moving car.

It is encouraging to learn that, despite road-building and other developments, Spiked Star-of-Bethlehem grows today in much the same places in which it was admired more than two centuries ago. For example, the third edition of John Ray's *Synopsis Methodica Stirpium Britannicarum* published in 1724 places it on a hill between Bristol and Bath, and 'in a Way between Bath and Bradford, not far from Little Ashley'. *The Flora of Somerset* rates it as locally abundant from Stockwood (south-east district of Bristol) to the Wiltshire border east of Bath, and *en route* for Bradford.

The *Synopsis* also describes the plants as growing 'on the left Hand of a Farm, half a Mile from Chichester, Southgate, in a Meadow plentifully'. It still grows plentifully next to a footpath by the side of a meadow, little more than a mile from Chichester, in the lane leading from Fishbourne to Dell Quay. It is also apt to turn up unexpectedly in new areas: around Greenham Common, just outside Newbury, for instance, and even in Scotland. It flowers from early June in the south, sometimes well into July.

Spring Cinquefoil (*Potentilla tabernaemontani*)

The plant was named in honour of Jacobus Theodorus (?1520–1590), a botanist who spent 36 years writing his famous work, *Neuw Kreuterbuch* (New Plantbook). He published its 3000 illustrations separately without text, under the title *Eicones Plantarum* (The Images of Plants), some of which reappeared in the first edition of Gerard's *Herbal*. Jacob Theodorus was a native of Bergzabern (meaning 'Hill-tavern') near Karlsruhe in Germany; scholars of the day Latinised this name to their satisfaction and latched it on to their sixteenth-century colleague.

This species is one of the Rose family and not far removed from the Strawberries. The flowers are $\frac{1}{2}$ inch or more in diameter, with five notched petals and the brilliant yellow colouring of a springtime flower. The stems are trailing, the plants mat-forming. The leaflets of the basal leaves are spread out like the five fingers of a glove.

The plant favours dry grassland on the chalk and rocky outcrops, particularly those on sunny slopes, but is very local and, though a chalk-lover, it must be one of the very few rarities passed over in J.E. Lousley's classic work *Wild Flowers of Chalk and Limestone*. It is said to be extinct in Suffolk where it was formerly well known. A dependable site over the past decade has been the same cliff below Durdham Down, Clifton, on which there are plants of *Hornungia* which flower about two weeks or more before the first week of April when the Spring Cinquefoil is due.

Spring Snowflake (*Leucojum vernum*)

The Spring Snowflake, to be visited towards the end of February, is not to be confused with the widely established Snowdrop, whose leaves are a mere 9 inches at most in height; those of the Spring Snowflake are double that size. Furthermore in the case of the Snowdrop the outer segments of the flower are longer than the inner; in the Snowflakes the two rings of segments are always the same size.

The Spring Snowflake is seldom, if ever, truly wild but gives a convincing impression of being so in at least two areas remote from houses or gardens. One site, dating from 1910, lies in Somerset about midway between Stogumber and Crowcombe above the Doniford stream, in a private wood, the owner of which should be approached through the Somerset Trust for Nature Conservation. The alternative site is at Wootton Fitzpaine, a few miles north-east of Lyme Regis in Dorset, where the plants were first recorded in 1866.

The flowers of the Spring Snowflake, usually one from each stalk (a feature which distinguishes them from those of the Summer Snowflake), are white and bell-shaped, with the outer segments tipped with green. During the early stages of flowering, the blossoms look skywards, perhaps to encourage pollination, but later, as seeding time approaches, the bells hang mouth downwards for, when the seeds fall, they will be transported by ants to a fresh seed-bed, a fairly successful, if localised, mode of propagation.

Three-cornered Leek (*Allium triquetrum*)

Three-cornered Leek rises to a height of 18 inches or more, and presents a cluster of drooping white bell-shaped flowers decorated internally with green lines. This is one of the species of garlic which survive without relying on bulbils (small bulbs grown with the flowers) for propagation. The stem, as the name implies, is three-cornered. The leaves are linear (that is, with the main edges more or less parallel) and keeled (rounded) beneath.

This graceful plant can be bought for the garden from bulb specialists, and was no doubt originally imported to decorate the flower-bed. It is a native of southern Spain, Portugal, Italy, Morocco and Tunisia, but is fully naturalised in parts of Britain.

It is to be found in Glamorgan, Pembrokeshire and Anglesey among other localities in Wales, and in the Channel Islands, where it is so common as to be rated as something of a pest. It also decorates walls on the Isles of Scilly. On the mainland it is most frequently seen in Cornwall (where it was first noticed in the latter half of the last century). There it peeps out from almost every bank and hedgerow. The Lizard peninsula is especially, but by no means exclusively, favoured. This is one of the rarer plants which is said to be on the increase, but some more years will have to pass before it becomes generally familiar to passers-by.

May and June are the months when the flowers are at their best.

Thyme Broomrape (*Orobanche alba*)

This parasitic species is distinguished in Britain by the fiery red of its stem and flowers, though this distinction does not, apparently, hold good on the European continent where, to judge by its botanical name, their colour must be white, or at least near-white. There is a strong suspicion that its host-plant is not invariably wild thyme, but could on occasion include other members of the same family.

At a height of – sometimes – 3–5 inches Thyme Broomrape is shorter than most other Broomrapes, and rather stouter. There is an abundance of purplish-red scales near the base of the stem. The flowers are relatively few, though large – up to $\frac{3}{4}$ inch – in proportion to the length of the stem, and are longer than the bracts immediately beneath them. The lips are curled, with three almost equal lobes to the lower lip.

Thyme Broomrape is at home on rock-strewn slopes in fairly remote areas of Britain – in North Skye, for instance, and the Inner and Outer Hebrides. It is also to be found on parts of the northern coast of Ireland and in Co. Clare in the west. So it is perhaps not asking too much to suggest to the botanist who wants to see this plant that he should look for it on the Lizard peninsula of Cornwall. There he should inspect the short turf on either side of the entrance to Kynance Cove. The Broomrape is in flower from June to August.

Tuberous Thistle (*Cirsium tuberosum*)

One of the main features which distinguishes this species – the rarest of our thistles – from others of its kind is the root, which is swollen and spindle-shaped. But since this peculiarity cannot be verified without digging up the plant, we have to rely on other details in order to establish its identity. Here are some of them.

In the first place, it has no stolons – short auxiliary surface roots – such as are possessed by the north-country Melancholy Thistle (*Cirsium heterophyllum*) and the Meadow Thistle (*Cirsium dissectum*). Its basal leaves are deeply cut, and green on both sides; the stem is grooved and cottony but unwinged; and the involucre, from which the dark, reddish-purple florets arise, is almost globe-shaped. Often the heads contain but a single flower. Amid long grass the plant can rise to 2½ feet.

In some older works, two localities only are mentioned: the military training area east of Westbury, and a doubtful site near Eversden in Cambridgeshire. Since then new sites have been discovered in Glamorgan and in Wiltshire, particularly on Wylye Down, close to the village of that name and near the crossroads between the A36 and the A303. This is a Nature Conservancy Council reserve and a permit is required from those wishing to leave the right of way over the down. In some areas there are persistent hybrids between the Tuberous Thistle and the very much smaller Stemless Thistle (*Cirsium acaule*). June to August are the flowering months.

*Viper's-grass (*Scorzonera humilis*)

This was known to sixteenth-century botanists as Viper's-grass not because it was attractive to vipers but because the apothecaries of the day believed that it was specific antidote to snake-bite. The description *humilis* meaning 'low-growing' referred to the fact that there were other, more resplendent Viper's-grasses abroad, in particular in Hungary and Austria.

It is not a grass at all, but a 6–12 inch, canary-flowered member of the Dandelion family. Of course there are many such plants: innumerable Hawkweeds, Hawkbits, Hawk's-beards, etc.; but this can be distinguished from all of them by the leaves, which arise almost from the base of the plant and are ribbed, narrow, uncut, tapering into a winged stalk which partially sheathes the base of the stem. The brilliant yellow florets are of unequal length, giving the flowers a somewhat starry appearance.

There is only one meadow in the whole of the British Isles where this plant can be seen in quantity and, as it is on private property, permission should be sought through the Nature Conservancy Council Office which, though in East Dorset, is administered from Taunton. The best display in this meadow is early in May, but later in the season, from July on, another rarity – Whorled Caraway (*Carum verticillatum*) – should be in flower, and it is just possible in some years to get the two together. Occasionally Viper's-grass has been known to seed itself casually in ditches in the Arne peninsula of Dorset.

*Water Germander (*Teucrium scordium*)

Here is a member of the Dead Nettle tribe which, like all
Germanders, has only one lip, the lower, which juts out forward
after the manner of a hound's tongue. Germander comes from two
Greek words meaning 'ground-oak', which may be appropriate in
the case of some under-shrubby Mediterranean Germanders, but not
to this species, which is softly hairy with shallow roots. The flowers,
on show between July and September, are of a delicate pink.

This species grows beside, rather than in, the water, on river-
banks, ditches, dykes and on the edges of gravel pits, but rarely
persists for long unless freed from the competition of more aggressive
plants. Records vary from year to year, but at the time of writing the
number of sites where this plant can be found appears to have sunk
to two. The first is in the Cambridgeshire fen country, particularly in
the area of Wicken Fen near Soham, a nature reserve in the care of
the National Trust, and near Stretham, 4 miles south-west of Ely.
There is always a chance that the plant may reappear in areas
which have been recently cleared for peat digging or for drainage.

In the west, the remaining sites are by ditches near the south-east
corner of Braunton Burrows, about 6 miles west of Barnstaple. This
is a Nature Conservancy Council reserve without restrictions except
in areas in use by the military. But in view of the retiring nature of
the plant, it is probably best to contact the local warden in advance
through the Nature Conservancy Council.

White Rock-rose (*Helianthemum apenninum*)

This, of course, is not the white form of the Common (yellow) Rock-rose but a species in its own right, and a very rare one. It differs from the Common Rock-rose in other ways than in the colour of the flower. Its leaves are narrower and the edges more decisively rolled back, and the upper surface is covered with a coating of dense greyish cottony hairs.

It does, indeed, flower on the Apennine mountains of Italy, but is equally at home elsewhere in western Europe. John Ray in his *Synopsis Methodica Stirpium Britannicarum* published in 1724 knew it as 'the Dwarf Cistus with Poley-mountain Leaves', adding that it had been found by Dr Plukenet 'upon Brent-Downs in Somersetshire near the Severn-Sea'.

It is still not far away – on Brean Down, that elevated finger that points out into the 'Severn-Sea' from Uphill, just to the south of Weston-super-Mare. This is a mere 2 miles away from another site on which the plant has been regularly recorded, namely Purn Hill, Bleadon. Brent Knoll, a hill-top visible for miles around, is another 4 miles to the south. But there is no need to search elsewhere than on Brean Down, where plants are abundant from May to July.

There is, however, an alternative west-country site on Berry Head, the limestone headland to the south of Torbay, in the reserve managed by Torbay Borough Council. Here the plant grows on limestone crags together with some other rarities seen nowhere else in such close company.

Wild Cabbage (*Brassica oleracea*)

The cabbage becomes a romantic-looking plant in its wild state, perched on the very edge of a cliff-top. Horticulturalists might despise the Wild Cabbage in flower, and accuse it of having 'bolted', or of being in danger of running uselessly to seed, but, to the field botanist, the plant appears tall and even graceful. The stems lengthen during the flowering process, with the new buds continuously overtopping the lemon-yellow flowers. Beneath is a ruff of leaves, broad, rounded and hairless with a hint of sea-green in them. Leaves and flowers are supported on a woody stem, disfigured by the scars left by earlier leaves.

Is the Wild Cabbage really a native plant? Or did the Romans, or the Celts before them, bring seed or plants with them to grow them for the pot? This species is well known as a native plant in other countries with a North Atlantic coastline including France, and there seems no sound reason for disestablishing it from, at least, the southern part of Britain, even if elsewhere 'Wild Cabbage' could be just a garden escape.

This photograph was taken in Dorset, below Worth Matravers, but there are other typically 'native' sites along the south coastline – as for instance around Dover, and on Afton Down Cliffs on the Isle of Wight where it was recorded in 1655 by the great botanist Mathias de l'Obel, after whom the Lobelia was named. In Wales, it flourishes on cliffs, particularly in Monmouthshire, Glamorgan, Dyfed and Gwynedd. Flowering time is from April to August.

AREA THREE: ISLES OF SCILLY

Balm-leaved Figwort (*Scrophularia scorodonia*)

Most of the plants in this sector of the Guide are rare on the mainland of Britain, but plentiful on the Isles of Scilly.

Balm-leaved Figwort is one of these. It is confined, as a native plant on the mainland, to local sites in parts of Devon (almost entirely in the area around Kingsbridge) and, in Cornwall, in the west near Hayle and further east at Padstow. In Glamorgan, it is an introduced plant.

On the Isles of Scilly, however, it is as common as the ordinary Figwort (*Scrophularia nodosa*) is rare, and can be discovered on marshy ground, in dunes, hedgerows and amid rocks. The most favoured locations, however, are near water, as for instance on the island of St Mary's in Holy Vale or by the water on Higher Moors, or on Tresco on the fringe of Abbey Pool. It is also fairly common on Bryher, St Martin's and St Agnes. Often, the new plants can be found growing close to withered specimens remaining from the previous year.

The leaves are one of the main distinguishing features of this plant. They are wrinkled, covered with fine, greyish down, and irregularly toothed. The stem is sharply four-angled, but not winged as is the case with Water Figwort (*Scrophularia auriculata*) and Green Figwort (*S. umbrosa*). The flowering season is June to August but marginally earlier in the Isles of Scilly.

Bermuda Buttercup (*Oxalis pes-caprae*)

This is not a Buttercup but a relative of the demure Wood sorrel which haunts the shadows of our woods in springtime. Nor is it especially connected with Bermuda, although it grows there (as it does also in countries around the Mediterranean). Its true home is in southern Africa.

The flowers, as much as an inch across, are brilliant yellow – the colour summer butter used to be. They are carried on leafless pedestals, from the tops of which the individual flower-stalks sprout like jets from a sprinkler. In dull weather the petals fold into inconspicuous pointed buds. The leaves are of the shamrock type, and are on stalks up to 8 inches long, held close to the ground. Seed is not normally produced in our climate, and the plants reproduce themselves by means of bulbils growing above and below ground level.

This is a rare plant on the mainland, and, being too tender to survive frosts, is to be found only in sheltered parts of Devon and Cornwall mainly in fields where bulbs have been grown. This is also the preferred habitat in the Isles of Scilly – especially in St Mary's, St Martin's and Tresco. The bulb growers have tried for years to get rid of the plants, but in many areas they have become established in the walls used as windbreaks around the bulb-fields and cannot be uprooted without damage to the stonework. The flowers appear from March to June.

Four-leaved Allseed (*Polycarpon tetraphyllum*)

This undistinguished member of the Pink family is usually described as 'rare' or even 'very rare' in waste sandy places as for instance on Chesil Beach in Dorset, near the mouth of the River Avon, near Kingsbridge in Devon, and as a casual in Cornwall. On the Isles of Scilly, however, it is comparatively common on walls and in bulb-fields, as well as on natural habitats such as dunes. It is also to be seen in quantity in the Channel Islands.

Four-leaved Allseed is a near-prostrate plant, seldom more than 4 inches long, with leaves in pairs each at right angles to the next, but so crowded together as to look as though they were disposed in whorls of four. The leaves are obovate, that is egg-shaped in outline but with the widest part furthest from the stalk. The sepals, hooded, sharply pointed and decorated with white or colourless margins, are more prominent than the white petals, which fall away early in the day.

While there are many sites from which to choose, one of the most easily accessible is on St Mary's, on the east side of Old Town Lane in the bulb-field which adjoins the A3110 leading eastwards. There are also plants on the walls near the Old Town church. Once the eye knows what to expect, acquaintance with the plant can be renewed on Tresco, Bryher, St Martin's and St Agnes. The flowers, such as they are, appear from May onwards.

Italian-Lords-and-Ladies (*Arum italicum*)

This species is quite distinct from the ordinary Lords-and-Ladies (*Arum maculatum*) – alias Cuckoo-pint or Jack-in-the-Pulpit) to be seen in countless country lanes in spring. This latter often has spotted leaves, sometimes wrinkled and with a dark green mid-rib; the spadix (central fleshy spike) is nearly always purple, and the bract (the 'pulpit') surrounding it is twice as long as the spadix and frequently edged with purple.

In the Italian Lords-and-Ladies, the fleshy spike is pale yellow, but the experts, in their wisdom, have chosen to divide this species into two sub-species, one of which, *Arum italicum*, sub-species *italicum*, is an imported alien with dark green, white-veined leaves attractive to gardeners. The other sub-species which concerns us here is a native plant, *Arum italicum, sb.sp. neglectum*. This, too, has a pale yellow spadix, but the surrounding bract is three times as long as the spadix and not edged with purple. The leaves are paler green, unwrinkled, unspotted and not white-veined. It is a rather larger plant than *A. maculatum* and flowers somewhat later, beginning May.

On the mainland, it is found sparingly in the south, usually not far from the sea, as for instance near Dinas Powys in Glamorgan, and in West Cornwall on the outskirts of Penzance, and near Hayle. On the Isles of Scilly, however, it is abundant, and the only native wild Arum to be seen. The banks of the narrow stream that wanders through Holy Vale on St Mary's is one of many haunts.

Orange Bird's-foot (*Ornithopus pinnatus*)

This little gem is a speciality of the Isles of Scilly, and at the time of writing had never been indisputably recorded on the British mainland, though it occurs in the Channel Islands on Alderney, Sark, Guernsey and Herm – though not Jersey.

Although it is a member of the Pea family, the flowers, in ones or twos together, and less than a third of an inch long, somewhat resemble bright orange trumpets pointing to the skies, with narrow mouths and jutting lower lips. The leaves are pinnate, with leaflets, even smaller than the flowers, in pairs along a common 'stalk', an arrangement which serves – need one say – to distinguish them from those of the Bird's-foot-trefoils with their clover-like leaves.

Orange Bird's-foot was discovered in April 1838 by Miss Matilda White on the island of Tresco which is its main home, though some former sites to the south of the Tresco helicopter pad have become sanded over and dried out after the winter storms of the '80s.

Orange Bird's-foot is an annual species, and the exact locations may vary from year to year, but one of the most dependable is on the sandy downs overlooking Merchant's Point, where, in recent years, there have been two large colonies. It is also to be found on Bryher, St Martin's and St Agnes, though not apparently on St Mary's.

Orange Bird's-foot begins to flower in April and continues into autumn unless previously burnt up by drought.

Prickly-fruited Buttercup (*Ranunculus muricatus*)

It is hardly surprising that the Isles of Scilly should have their own special buttercup, though it remained unnoticed there until 1923. As the name implies, the distinguishing feature of this species is the achenes, the single-seeded fruits of which each flower can produce up to a dozen or more. Each achene is equipped on both faces with a number of short spines, each proceeding from a prominent 'beak' almost half the length of the rest of the achene.

The lower leaves are on long stalks, shallow-lobed, and roundish in general outline, and the stems rising to a height of 18 inches or so are much-branched, spreading or climbing over the surrounding vegetation.

The species was originally of Mediterranean origin, but has spread to both east and west coasts of North America and to Australia and New Zealand. In Britain it is established not only in the Isles of Scilly but also on the Cornish mainland near Gulval and at Poltesco on the Lizard.

It raises problems for the bulb-growers because it rises and flowers at the same time as the crop and has already dropped its seeds before the fields come to be cleared. It is abundant in the fields in the southern half of St Mary's and to a lesser extent in the north of the island, where this photograph was taken. It is also to be seen on St Agnes and Bryher but is not much evident – yet – on St Martin's.

Small-flowered Catchfly (*Silene gallica*)

Here is one of those species which used to be common enough on the edges of mainland cornfields, and on waste ground, but which has become local and decreasing in numbers possibly because of excessive spraying, road-widening and other development. It is however still abundant in the Isles of Scilly, and whereas in Britain the flowers are usually either dingy white or even yellowish, the petals of the flowers on the islands are usually either clear white, or suffused with pink.

Occasionally, the 'five-wounds' variety, *Silene gallica, var. quinque vulnera*, so called because of the dark red spot at the base of each petal, occurs in the wild, and is enthusiastically cultivated from seed in Scillonian gardens. However, as in the Channel Islands, the 'wounds' sometimes extend to the point where only a narrow white edging remains at the borders of the petals.

The normal white and pink forms are, however, interesting enough. Normally the plants are erect, but where a dozen or so grow together in a clump, the stems of the outer ones are partially decumbent. The flowers all favour the same side of the stem, but are inclined alternately to the right and to the left. The petals are but slightly, if at all, notched, and each calyx is decorated with fine black ribs.

There should be no need to search for Small-flowered Catchfly on the bulb-fields themselves, as they tend to grow mainly in the headlands. The flowers appear from May onwards.

Smaller Tree Mallow (*Lavatera cretica*)

The Smaller Tree Mallow is rare and sporadic on the British mainland, and is seen only in western Cornwall and South Wales. On the Isles of Scilly, however, it is not too difficult to find it on waste ground, in quarries or against stone walls, flowering usually during May and early June. One usually dependable location is on the island of St Mary's by the walls of the Old Town itself and in the bulb-field lying between the Old Town and its church.

The plant is at home in the Mediterranean – including Crete – but is also found in western Europe. In Brittany it grows in habitats similar to those which it occupies in the Isles of Scilly, and it is thus held to be a native plant at least in the extreme west of Britain.

The Smaller Tree Mallow is readily distinguished from the (common) Tree Mallow (*Lavatera arborea*) which is essentially a shrub with a woody stem. It can also be told apart from the Common Mallow (*Malva sylvestris*), the flowers of which often open out flat to show purplish petals striped with darker purple. The flowers of the Smaller Tree Mallow on the other hand are close to a china-white, striped with pale mauve or lilac (not pink as is sometimes averred). The sides of the petals are nearly parallel (not curved as is the case with the Common Mallow), and the flowers are shy about opening fully. (The petals roll together into a cone when either the weather or the light does not suit).

Western Fumitory (*Fumaria occidentalis*)

We return here to a native species which is unknown on the mainland outside Cornwall, or indeed anywhere else in the world, but is relatively common in bulb-fields and walls of St Mary's in the Isles of Scilly.

Telling one species of Fumitory from another is often a matter to be determined by experts alone, but Western Fumitory is distinctive enough for it to be identified almost at first sight. Indeed it was surprising that it was not identified on the Isles of Scilly until 1937. It is larger and more substantial than the commoner species of Fumitory: not so recumbent, more of a climber, and more erect. When fresh, the flowers are essentially white, turning to pink or red only when past their best. The blackish-red wings of the upper petals of the flowers are bordered with white edging, and the lower petals are strap-like, widening towards the tip.

In Cornwall it is confined almost entirely to the western half of the county, having been recorded at Land's End, Upton Towans and Mullion and Cadgwith Bay in the Lizard area, and Newquay. In the Isles of Scilly it is apparently confined to St Mary's, and one easily reached site there lies on the left-hand side of Old Town Lane leading northwards from the Old Town towards Rocky Hill. To reach this site, proceed northward to a point beyond the turning to the Heliport, but short of the east-west T-junction, and examine the upper part of the wall. It flowers from May through to October.

AREA FOUR: EAST ANGLIA

Berry Catchfly (*Cucubalus baccifer*)

This interesting species – peculiar, it is believed, to Norfolk – has been persistently recorded there, in and around the village of Merton. It sprawls, rather after the style of Traveller's Joy, the wild Clematis, over and above hedges, and scrambles across bushes in open copses. The greenish-white flowers are bell-shaped, and the petals deeply cleft, with points turned upwards and outwards. In the midst of each flower a large, black, shining, globe-shaped berry eventually forms.

When he saw these berries and learnt that they were the preferred food of the pheasants of Hungary – where the plant is native – an ancestor of the Walsingham family decided to bring back some specimens with him and had them planted in woods on the family estate at Merton, where they still flourish. It was not until 1914 that the plant was noticed by a botanist, Mr Fred Robinson, who thought for a time that he had discovered the only site for a native species new to Britain.

From the 1960s onwards, new sites have been discovered near Merton at Broadflash Farm, and at Hills and Holes (the one near Great Hockham). Another reliable site is along the hedges bordering Sparrow Hill Lane which branches west from the minor road connecting Merton with the village of Thompson to join the old Roman road known as Peddars Way. No doubt the pheasants will see to it that other new sites materialise in future. Wait till mid-August to see the flowers.

Crested Cow-wheat (*Melampyrum cristatum*)

Despite its densely flowered spike, rose-purple toothed bracts, and yellow and purple flowers this plant is not as conspicuous among the summer grasses as one might suppose, and it is in any case more or less confined to the edges of woods and roadside verges of a few eastern counties – in particular where the soil is boulder clay.

One site is near the borders of Southey Wood some 5 miles to the west of Peterborough in north Cambridgeshire. Two further sites in Cambridgeshire are at Hatley and at Hardwick to the west of the city of Cambridge. Another site is on the eastern verge of a lane west of St Neots, which joins the village of Honeydon, in a zig-zag manner, with Begwary. Do not pursue this lane southward further than the sharp right-angled turn leading to Colmworth. Another well-attested site is at Great Hormead, a few miles west of Saffron Walden, and plants have also been recorded nearby in the lanes around Little Chishill.

Further north in Suffolk, plants can be found in the area 5 miles to the west of Bury St Edmunds by taking the lane running south from the village of Barrow and pausing at the crossroads about $\frac{1}{2}$ mile north of Hargrave to look in the north-west quadrant of that junction. It should be borne in mind that Crested Cow-wheat is an annual, appearing in varying numbers, and does best in woods or hedgerows that have recently been cleared. It flowers from late June to mid-August.

Cypress Spurge (*Euphorbia cyparissias*)

Less than a foot tall, the Cypress Spurge is nevertheless full of character. The plants spring from a creeping underground root or rhizome, so that they often appear in groups close together. The leaves, unstalked and needle-thin, are closely packed and the shoots in the early stages of growth suggest a sweep's brush about to enter the chimney. But, later, the flowers and their stalks spread out far and wide beyond the central stalk as the sweep's brush would after it has overtopped the chimney.

The flowers are a brilliant gold and, after flowering, the heads turn to an equally brilliant red. Though it is popular with gardeners, the general impression is that Cypress Spurge is a native plant at least in some areas. It is a lover of dry chalk grassland particularly in the eastern part of the country and is generally accepted as native there.

Some observers however have noted that Cypress Spurge seems to show a partiality for localities where racehorses are trained. In Surrey it has been recorded on Walton Down, near Epsom. It has also been found on Newmarket Heath and, in Suffolk, on Tuddenham Gallops, a mile west of the village of that name. Whether the hooves of the racehorses encourage the plant by compacting the turf, or whether the seeds of Cypress Spurge occur regularly in fodder imported for racehorses, is unclear.

Some books give late May as the date when flowering commences, but this picture was taken at Tuddenham in mid-April.

Dusky Cranesbill (*Geranium phaeum*)

While this plant often vaults the garden wall in order to take up residence on a suitable sunny bank, it is equally to be found on sites remote from houses. The great Linnaeus in his *Flora Anglica* of 1754 treated it as a wild plant, and so too, 200 years later, did J.E. Dandy in his *List of British Vascular Plants* prepared for the British Museum (Natural History) and the Botanical Society of the British Isles.

In the hedgerow the plant looks as though it naturally belongs there – partly, perhaps, because the flowers, so much darker than most, look particularly unassuming. However, Dusky Cranesbill is intolerant of competition and by no means always persists on sites in the wild: hence the records of past appearances offer no guarantees for the future.

These records are, however, spread far and wide across the country. Thus in Mary McCallum Webster's valuable *Flora of Moray, Nairn and East Inverness* Dusky Cranesbill was said to be 'well established a few yards north of Earnhill, Kintessack', on the edge of Culbin Forest 3 miles west of Forres, and to occur on waste ground at Forres. Another record comes from Upper Wasdale in Cumbria. There have been at least 60 records at various times in Wales. In Essex, it became naturalised in the castle grounds of Castle Hedingham, near Halstead, and the botanist John Raven has written of a large colony on the verges of the road leading from Cambridge on to the Gog and Magog Hills. Look in May and June.

*(Great) Fen Ragwort (*Senecio paludosus*)

Once upon a time, the Great Fen Ragwort was found in ditches in
East Anglia, particularly those of Cambridgeshire, Norfolk and
Suffolk. But *Simpson's Flora of Suffolk* stated that there had been no
records for the plant in Suffolk this century and that it had last been
seen in about 1850 in Lakenheath Fen near Wangford. Similarly,
according to Dr C.P. Petch and E.L. Swann's *Flora of Norfolk*, the last
Norfolk record came in 1835 from Redmore Fen adjoining the Little
Ouse at Brandon. *A Flora of Cambridgeshire* by J.H. Perring, P.D. Sell
and S.M. Walters stated without equivocation: 'This plant . . . is now
extinct in the British Isles.' It was an understandable assumption in
an area where fens were being extensively drained.

But a surprise was in store for the pessimists, for in 1972 a group
of Great Fen Ragwort plants was rediscovered in Cambridgeshire in
a ditch so deep that, when in it, one's head is level with the tread of
tractor tyres bouncing along the road a few yards away. Thus the
6-foot plant and its narrow, saw-toothed leaves would be invisible
from the highway.

Take the A142 road running north-west from Soham, and shortly
after the turning to Eye Hill Farm, look on the left-hand side for a
lay-by. Draw into this, and investigate the ditch on the far side of the
road you have just left. To avoid treading on plants not yet in
flower, do not start looking before mid-August.

Fritillary (*Fritillaria melaegris*)

At one time there was some doubt as to whether this chequered member of the lily family was a native plant, for it was not discovered in the wild in Britain until well into the eighteenth century. However it flowers in sites where it is unlikely to have been planted, and in water-meadows of the kind that it frequents on the continent of Europe. So: 'native' it is and flowering in mid-April.

A tributary of the River Deben in Suffolk is the setting for the 6-acre Fox Fritillary Meadow at Framsden, bought by the Suffolk Trust for Nature Conservation from the executors of Mrs B. ('Queenie') Fox, who with her family preserved the Fritillaries for decades by letting people see them for a small charge. A count in the 1980s put the population (of Fritillaries) there at nearly 50,000 plants to the acre.

The Fritillary also frequents the Thames Valley. There is a well-known site at the Duke of Wellington's home at Stratfield Saye, close to the River Loddon. There is also the gigantic unimproved North Meadow just outside Cricklade. Here, as at Stratfield Saye, two forms of Fritillary are to be seen, the dull purplish-red, and the greenish-white. Further upstream, near the source of the Thames at Trewsbury Meadow, one may hope with the farmer's leave to discover Fritillaries as they really should be seen: flowering in the smaller water-meadows while the wind stirs the willows close behind.

Grape Hyacinth (*Muscari neglectum (atlanticum)*)

This species is entirely distinct from the neon-blue cultivars to be seen in gardens and, quite often, as an escape from them. The wild plant (to be seen also from the Mediterranean northwards to Germany and Belgium) is shorter and plumper than the garden captives, and the flowers range from slate blue at the top of the spike to dark purple lower down. They really do suggest a bunch of grapes.

It is most at home on chalk or limestone, on permanent grassland, where it persists if the grass is kept short by rabbits, grazing or judicious mowing. There is one such site on waste ground close to allotments at a Cotswold village north-west of Oxford.

But East Anglia is its true home. In Suffolk it is to be found on the headland of an arable field shielded by pine trees at Tuddenham Gallops, a mile to the west of the village of that name, on a grid reference of 722-715. There are also a number of roadside nature reserve verges specially maintained to suit the wild Grape Hyacinth. They are marked with white posts inscribed NR. Two of these reserves are on both sides of the road at Tuddenham with grid references 730-718 and 729-720. Other verge sights are at Culford – grid references 823-713 and 828-712 (both north side) and 828-716 (west side). In Cambridge the traditional site is between Cherry Hinton and the Gog and Magog Hills.

The flowers are at their best in late March and early April.

Hoary Mullein (*Verbascum pulverulentum*)

No other Mullein is endowed with so much mealy white fluff as this one: it covers the stem, and both sides of the leaves, which helps to distinguish it from both the Great Mullein (*Verbascum thapsus*) and the White Mullein (*Verbascum lychnitis*).

At 4 feet, the Hoary Mullein is shorter than the Great Mullein and the flowers are smaller, but it looks more stately and imposing; for the branches carrying the flowers stand well apart from the main stem, causing the whole plant to look somewhat pyramidal in shape and even rather like a Christmas tree.

Although it is regarded as a native plant, Hoary Mullein was not recorded as a separate species till 1745, when it was found in a ditch bounding the walls of Norwich city. It is very much a local plant of Norfolk, and, to a lesser degree, of Suffolk, and is hardly found elsewhere except as a casual. It frequently becomes established on the broad roadside grass verges which characterise parts of East Anglia, as well as on waste ground, railway cuttings, river-banks, and even in car-parks.

Where, as often happens, there are groups of several plants growing together, they can easily be detected from behind the driving wheel. A typical example is furnished by a colony of handsome plants on the western verge of the A149, heading north from King's Lynn, just beyond the turning on to a by-road leading to Sandringham. The flowers appear from mid-July onwards into August.

Maiden Pink (*Dianthus deltoides*)

The flowers are smaller, much darker, and redder than those of its nearest cousin, the Cheddar Pink, and the petals are narrower and well separated from one another. Each is fretted at the outer edge, and the centre of the flower is white, marked round with an irregular circle of darker red. Many non-flowering bluish-green shoots recline along the ground. This species is perennial.

Maiden Pink is frequently on offer at nurseries as being suitable for rock-gardens or crazy paving, which is logical since the plant insists on a dry situation. Consequently, though there are sites in Wales, it is less often to be seen in the west of the country where the rainfall is more copious. It also shows a partiality for golf courses – where the grass is kept comparatively short, and the greens are sprinkled from time to time with sand from the surrounding bunkers.

Cambridgeshire has one locality for this plant – originally discovered by John Ray in 1685 – at Hildersham Furze Hills, off the A1307, leading to the A604 south-east from Cambridge; and there are a handful of sites in Norfolk, almost all in the west of the county. But the plant is far more at home in Suffolk. There, the best-known locality is on sand in the neighbourhood of West Stow Heath, easily reached from Bury St Edmunds travelling north-west along the A1101 towards Wisbech, and taking a left turn after having crossed the River Lark. There are other sites at Icklingham and Cavenham Heath. Maiden Pink is in flower from June to September.

*Military Orchid (*Orchis militaris*)

The sepals of the Military Orchid grow together to form a whitish, metallic-looking, pale lilac 'helmet' which completely hides the upper petals. It could be this feature, or perhaps the two parallel rows of spotted 'tunic-buttons', lower down on the lip, that have led to the orchid's enrolment in the ranks of some Ruritanian regiment.

There are still a half-handful of sites for the Military Orchid in the Chilterns, in the woods north-east of Henley, and serious botanists are sometimes taken to one of them to see, on a bank outside the wood, orchids that have spread over from inside. This site was discovered by J.E. Lousley in 1947, more than 20 years after the Military Orchid was supposed to have become extinct: an example to us all never to give up looking for 'extinct' species.

Then in 1954 yet another colony of Military Orchids came to light, miles away in Suffolk. This site is in the midst of a wood and, but for this discovery, all the orchids would probably soon have died from light-starvation. Today, they are within the Rex Graham Reserve, watched over by the Suffolk Trust for Nature Conservation and surrounded by a high, all-but-unclimbable fence. Once a year, however, the reserve is opened for a day to serious botanists, who thread their way along a wooden board-walk – and leave it at their peril. A small charge is levied on photographers.

Oxlip (*Primula elatior*)

Let us first make some distinctions. Oxlip flowers are paler than those of the Primrose, which mounts each flower on a separate stem. They are larger and more widely open than the Cowslips and the flowers all point more or less in the same direction, which is not so in the case of the false Oxlip, a hybrid between the Primrose and the Cowslip.

The true Oxlip is confined to East Anglia in woods where the soil is boulder clay, that is clay that at one time had been rolled along and compressed by roving glaciers. Bradfield Woods, about 4 miles south-east from Bury St Edmunds, is one well-known site. These woods, which appear on older Ordnance Survey Maps as Felshamhall Wood and Monkspark Wood, can be reached by taking the A134 and branching off it at Sicklesmere towards, but not as far as, Gedding. They are managed by the Suffolk Trust for Nature Conservation; visitors are asked to keep to the rides and footpaths.

Elsewhere in East Anglia, there is a wide choice of privately owned small woods in which Oxlips flower. However, there is one site comparatively close to London, where Oxlips can be seen from a public footpath. Take the B1383 northwards from Bishop's Stortford towards the village of Quendon from which a footpath runs eastwards. After about a third of a mile, the path turns to the right along the edge of Quendon Wood. Try mid-April to May.

Sickle Medick (*Medicago sativa subsp. falcata*)

The purists regard this as a yellow-flowered form of Lucerne, the purple fodder plant which often persists in waste places after cultivation there has ceased. The main distinction between these two Medicks (colour apart) is, however, in the shape of the pods, which, in the case of Sickle Medick, are predictably, though not invariably, sickle-shaped. It is found only on grassland on gravelly soil in the Breckland.

For the average onlooker, however, the excitement comes not from the standard plant but from the extraordinary palette of colours that occur when Sickle Medick is crossed, and perhaps back-crossed, with Lucerne. Here in a single morning it is possible to see flowers coloured mauve, pink, yellow, green, blue, or almost black, the colour selected here. Botanically these hybrids are often lumped together under the title *Medicago falcata* × *M. sativa*.

The simplest method of finding a good selection of wayside Breckland plants is, as mentioned elsewhere to join the Suffolk Trust for Nature Conservation, and obtain from them a Handbook of Reserves. This contains a list of roadside verges maintained by the County Council Highways Department in liaison with the Suffolk Trust. These roadside nature reserves are marked with white posts inscribed NR to show the extent of the reserve and to aid the Highways Department to follow the recommended cutting regime.

Sickle Medick and its hybrids are in flower in June and July.

Spanish Catchfly (*Silene otites*)

The Breckland of East Anglia marks the north-west frontier for this species from the Steppes. Travel a few miles further west and the climate would be too damp for it, at any rate on a long-term basis. Spanish Catchfly needs open country and shallow quick-drying chalky soil of the kind on which the grass will stay thin and short. Rabbits can be a help, especially if they disturb the ground and create bare patches on which the seeds can germinate.

The plant is but a foot high, with small, delicate-looking greenish-white flowers springing from the end of short stalks in crowded clusters of four or five. The petals are as narrow as a fly's wing and the stamens of the male flowers (on different plants from the female) project prominently outwards giving the whole plant a 'busy', even insectiferous look. The paddle-shaped leaves are in pairs opposite one another.

There are perhaps half a dozen sites for this plant in Suffolk – one of them on Tuddenham Heath. Barton Mills, to the north of Tuddenham, is a well-attested site and Icklingham, 7 miles north-west of Bury St Edmunds, is another. The marked road verges around Icklingham are good sites for a number of other Breckland specialities.

In Norfolk, Barnham Heath, 3 miles south of Thetford, is the site most often shown to visitors, courtesy of the warden, through the Norfolk Naturalists' Trust. The flowers are on show from late June to late July.

AREA FIVE: WALES

Chives (*Allium schoenoprasum*)

Seen more often in the salad bowl than in the countryside, the Chive is nevertheless a truly native wild plant which has chosen for centuries to grow where it chooses – on the thinnest of soil, often on limestone, in remote rocky areas.

Viewed in their prime against a background of green grass, the flower heads sway to and fro above the herbage of like glowing fire-balls, and it is worth a day's journey to see them. The visit should be undertaken early in the flowering season, before the colours begin to fade towards a dusky purple. Early June is probably best although the flowers may start later, and last longer, in their northern stations. Chives are to be distinguished from that other rarity, the Round-headed Leek (*Allium sphaerocephalon*), whose stamens overtop the rest of the flower.

Wales, the land of the Leek, is where the Chive, a member of the same 'family', is most at home. There, the best-known sites are im Pembrokeshire near St David's, as, for instance, on grassland near the cliffs above Caer Bwdy Bay. Inland sites include one in Carmarthenshire at Carreg Cennen, where there is a spectacular outcrop of carboniferous limestone, and there are others on stone ledges along the banks of the Wye between Erwood, near Builth Wells, and Llyswen, where the river turns eastwards.

Cornwall is the other main area for Chives. On the north coast they grow on the rocks around Tintagel, and, in the south on Goonhilly Downs and on cliffs between Kynance Cove and Mullion.

*Early Star-of-Bethlehem (*Gagea bohemica*)

When still in bud, the flowers of this species resemble crocuses of brilliant yellow, lavishly striped outside with green. At this stage the petals are still hooded together at the top, as if two canary-coloured sedan chairs had been placed face to face. When the six petals (eight have been known), pointed, but not sharply so, first start to separate and the flower begins to open, it takes the form of a gentian or perhaps the body of a golden trumpet. But finally the petals lie open, wide apart, totally relaxed and star-like.

The leaves take two forms. From the base of the plant, two to four hair-like green threads rise up and curl, Medusa-fashion, in an intractable, thicket-like wreath round the plant – a useful shield, one might suppose, against the frosts of winter. The stem bears hoary greyish leaves of a different type: as straight, flat and pointed as a sword.

The story of the discovery of this species, previously unknown in Britain and found growing on Stanner Rocks near Kington in Powys in 1965, has been told elsewhere. Stanner Rocks is now a Nature Conservancy Council Reserve, and there are good reasons for not attempting to visit it without a permit from that body. The date and length of the flowering period is not to be relied on, and local advice is needed if disappointment is to be avoided. The terrain, though small, comprises a surprisingly large number of sheer precipices, and areas of bare rock with skating possibilities. And there are no mountain rescue facilities at hand.

*Fen Orchid (*Liparis loeselii*)

There are two distinct forms of the wispy, straw-coloured Fen Orchid, each worthy of separate study. The original Fen Orchid, so named when the species was thought to grow only in East Anglia, is a plant with leaves about four times as long as broad. It is still to be found occasionally on the edges of very wet fens at a certain stage in their development. However it is unable to compete with the intrusion of Reeds (*Phragmites communis*), which must be cut back annually if the flowers are to reappear. The water-level too has to be controlled so that it remains unaffected by that of the surrounding areas. There have been only intermittent records from its former haunts in Cambridgeshire, Suffolk and Norfolk, though encouraging reports have come in the past from Dilham, 5 miles south-east of North Walsham, near Norwich.

In the Welsh form (sometimes known as var. *ovata*) the leaves are broader in proportion and more suited, in appearance at least, to the designation *Liparis* meaning 'greasy'. Whereas 'eastern' *Liparis* grows in neutral or even slightly alkaline waters, western *Liparis* is often found on dune-slacks with Creeping Willow (*Salix repens*), which prefers acid soil. Here the dune-slacks of the Kenfig Nature Reserve are the site to make for – although there are other dune sites in Carmarthen. It is advisable to ring the Kenfig Reserve in advance, through the Mid-Glamorgan County Council, as the flowering time is variable and the plants are on easily compressed soil. A good week in July is best.

Hoary Rock-rose (*Helianthemum canum*)

Minor details, taken together, clearly distinguish this species from its closest cousin the Common Rock-rose (*Helianthemum chamaecistus*) which greets us on so many grassy chalk slopes.

The Hoary Rock-rose is of smaller stature (usually less than 8 inches) and has smaller flowers ($\frac{3}{8}$–$\frac{5}{8}$ inch in diameter) and smaller leaves (less than $\frac{1}{2}$ inch long) than the Common Rock-rose. It is also without stipules – the small scales that grow, most often, from the base of leaf-stalks. There is generally more silvery hair on the plant, as for instance on the sepals, and the style – the female organ in the centre of the flower – is not vertical but faintly S-shaped.

There are three main sites in Britain for the Hoary Rock-rose. One is in Teesdale, Co. Durham, and involves a somewhat dreary walk uphill through the heather, towards Cronkley Scar and an enclosed patch of sugar limestone within which the plants are on view. These Teesdale plants constitute a sub-species of Hoary Rock-rose, ssp. *levigatum*, distinguished by the leaves, which are dark green and almost hairless above. The accompanying photograph, however, is of the other sub-species, *Helianthemum canum ssp. canum*, which stands more erect, with hairier leaves and more flowers. The picture was taken on the Great Orme, not far from the houses which circle the base of the rock. There are other sites on the Gower peninsula and on Humphrey Head, at the northern corner of Morecambe Bay. The plants flower in June and July, and occasionally earlier.

Oyster plant (*Mertensia maritima*)

This appetising title was bestowed on the plant by someone who must have thought that the leaves tasted of oysters. But this sea-shore *Mertensia* is so seldom seen that one hesitates to take even a tentative nip out of its fleshy leaves.

The Oyster plant could logically have been included in the Scottish section of the book, where most of the sites occur (the best-known being at Auchenmalg Bay, near Glenluce). However, since many botanists might find it more convenient to visit North Wales than the remoter areas of Scotland, the plant is included here. The beach at Abergele – to be inspected on both sides after crossing over the railway bridge – is the latest recorded site. It is certainly somewhat depressing to see such fine plants with deep blue flowers and sea-green foliage lying there stark and uncared for, surrounded by plastic bottles and sweet papers. Yet one could argue that the plants would probably be more at risk if more people realised that they were looking at an Oyster plant than would be the case if they were kept in ignorance of it being a rarity.

This species is becoming progressively more scarce, yet it does from time to time turn up on new sites as unaccountably as it disappears from old ones. Could the nutlet seeds, perhaps, be sea-borne?

Expect to see flowers on the Welsh site at the end of June, and as late as August, probably, in Scotland.

250

*Rock Cinquefoil (*Potentilla rupestris*)

A wild strawberry might show some resemblance to this species, if it grew erect to 18 inches and produced white flowers up to $\frac{1}{2}$ inch across.

Nearly all the truly native sites for this rare and distinctive plant are in Wales. Edward Llwyd found it some three centuries ago on 'Craig Wreidhin', in the county of 'Montis Gomerici', where it still survives, even though part of today's Breidden Hill is being quarried for road-building. For some time after Llwyd's discovery the plants remained fairly plentiful, but their numbers dwindled alarmingly as nineteenth-century collectors climbed all but the most inaccessible parts of the rock. After World War II a small reserve was set up on the north side of the hill and replanted with seedlings from the original wild stock. Unfortunately the experiment failed and efforts have since been concentrated on the south-west part of the hill, with willing co-operation from the quarrymen, who have agreed to leave untouched a large rock-face to which the plants still cling. Seven of the original colony of plants were counted and logged by NCC men on climbing ropes in 1987.

At the other Welsh site on the banks of the River Wye, the future of the plants and that of the botanists who want to see them is equally insecure, for the river has become a day and night battle-ground in a war between water-bailiffs and salmon poachers. There is also a permanent risk of the plants being washed away during the serious flooding to which the river is subject. Nevertheless, try the first week in June.

*Snowdon Lily (*Lloydia serotina*)

It is a 6-inch white lily, striped obscurely with dark red or purplish veins, and Snowdonia is its only site in Britain. Edward Lloyd or, as he preferred it, Llwyd found it, though not in flower, in time for it to be included in the second edition of Ray's *Synopsis Methodica Stirpium Britannicarum* published in 1696.

Since then, botanists have risked their lives for a close-up view. Llwyd reported finding it 'on the highest rocks of Snowdon', which implies that there could be at least a third site other than the two normally visited by botanical sightseers. The best-known of these is not on Snowdon itself, but in the area variously described as the Glyders, Cwm Idwal or the Devil's Kitchen. This area which is a National Nature Reserve, is separated from Snowdon proper by the road running between Llanberis and Capel Curig.

There is no shortage of Alpines there: Mossy and Starry Saxifrages, Northern Rock-cress and, where there is shelter, the Wood Anemone. But all these show white flowers that are confusing to the eyes of anyone searching for the white chalices and spidery leaves of *Lloydia*. And without steep climbing there is no close acquaintance with any of them.

The alternative site, about which, perhaps, it might be unwise to be too precise, involves no rigorous climbing and is not on 'the highest rocks of Snowdon'. Indeed those that have eyes to see can admire the plants without ever leaving one of the less frequented tracks. The plant has a short flowering season, and the first week of June is normally correct.

*Spiked Speedwell (*Veronica spicata*)

Spires of blue allow these plants to be picked out from afar, as for instance in the Avon Gorge above Bristol, where a sidelong glance from the cliff-top suggests an array of blue candles decorating a Christmas tree.

The experts recognise two subspecies of Spiked Speedwell. The first of these, namely *Veronica spicata, ssp. spicata*, grows on the dry grassland of Norfolk, Suffolk and Cambridgeshire where it is becoming increasingly rare. The second, *Veronica spicata ssp. hybrida*, is a west-country plant growing, as we have seen, in Avon but also on limestone and volcanic rocks in Wales, including parts of Pembrokeshire, the Gower peninsula and the Great Orme – on a bank above the miniature golf course, where the accompanying photograph was taken. Further north it reappears on Humphrey Head to the north of Morecambe Bay.

Size seems to be the principal difference between these two subspecies, for the Breckland plants are a foot tall or less, whereas the western type can be twice as large and carries leaves that narrow abruptly before joining the leaf-stalk. One is, perhaps, entitled to wonder whether this last refinement is important enough to warrant the creation of two separate subspecies, particularly since the larger size of the western plants could be due to the wetter climate and basic soil in which they grow rather than to genetic factors.

Both types have a comparatively long flowering season, commencing in July and continuing into September.

Spotted Rock-rose (*Tuberaria guttata*)

There are two subspecies to be considered here: one is *T.guttata ssp. guttata* which is a native of the Mediterranean and unknown in Britain outside the Channel Islands. The other subspecies (some would say 'variety') is *T. guttata ssp. breweri*. This is unknown outside Britain and, at a height of 4 inches or less, is about one third the size of its Channel Islands cousin. There are some five stations for it in Anglesey, and, on the mainland, one at the tip of the Lleyn peninsula, in Gwynedd. It was discovered, probably in 1727, by the same Samuel Brewer who originally found the Cheddar Pink.

The plant is highly attractive, with petals of deep yellow, blotched, usually, with chocolate in the centre. The fact that it is an annual does, however, provide some protection since it is of no permanent value to a collector even if he were optimistic enough to suppose that it might grow anywhere else than on its wind-swept sea-girt rocks. Furthermore, the stems are weak, and the petals often fall to the ground on the very morning they have opened, which should discourage any flower arrangers from including them in a bouquet.

One place to look when on Anglesey is in the neighbourhood of footpaths above the South Stack Lighthouse in the north-west of the island, where an almost continuous stream of sightseers and hill-walkers ensures protective publicity. The very end of May is the time to begin looking – early in the morning, of course.

Sticky Catchfly (*Lychnis viscaria*)

This is probably the stickiest of all our Catchflies; the black bands on the stem beneath each pair of leaves represent viscid glandular 'no-go' areas for ants and other insects that would otherwise climb up to raid the nectar. The soft, yet glowing cerise lipstick of the flower petals puts to shame the red of such flowers as the Red Campion, the Ragged Robin and even the Corncockle. It is a plant of basic mineral-rich rocks.

Thomas Willisel, the original finder of Nottingham Catchfly, discovered Sticky Catchfly in 1660 on Samson's Ribs above Edinburgh where it still flowers. Edward Llwyd found it on the same Breidden Rock in Montgomeryshire where he had come across Rock Cinquefoil. But it is also to be seen on Stanner Rocks, a site discussed previously in connection with the Early Star-of-Bethlehem. (Unfortunately the two flowers cannot be seen there together at the same time, as the Sticky Catchfly begins to flower at the end of May.) At this last site, the numbers have increased considerably since wire fencing was placed round one of the main colonies to prevent grazing by sheep. Time will tell whether the sheep will have to be brought back later to protect the plants from competitive grasses.

Sticky Catchfly occurs sparingly on other rocky sites in Scotland: in Kirkcudbrightshire, Roxburghshire, Midlothian, Stirlingshire and Perthshire. The plant is also available from a number of nurseries, some of them offering a white form which occasionally occurs also in the wild.

*Wild Cotoneaster (*Cotoneaster integerrimus*)

The three Cotoneasters most often seen outside gardens are all importations. The Wall Cotoneaster (*C. horizontalis*) came to us from Western China, 'Rockspray' (*C. microphyllus*) from the Himalayas and *C. simonsii* sometimes called Himalayan Cotoneaster from Assam. So Wild Cotoneaster remains our only native species. It is by no means exclusive to Britain: it occurs on the continent of Europe from the Baltic to the Mediterranean, and from Central Spain to beyond the bounds of Europe as far as Iran.

In this country, however, it is very much a rarity, and is found on only one location: Great Orme's Head, near Llandudno, and in very small quantity even there. Indeed the *British Red Data Book*, compiled by F.H. Perring and L. Farrell and published in 1983 to assess the prospects for our rarer plants, put the number of survivors at four. Even those continue to exist largely because they are out of reach of, or inconveniently placed for, grazing sheep. Two are on rocks not far above the houses on the lower brow of the slope, another is near the very north of the headland, a gentle climb up from the road, and the fourth is in a relatively inaccessible position on one of the walls of the cemetery on a grid reference of approximately 768-838.

This woody shrub, when in exposed positions, is rarely more than 3 feet high; the leaves, more circular than oval and rounded at the base, are hairless above and densely coated below with short grey cottony hairs. The pinkish flowers come in April and May.

Yellow Whitlowgrass (*Draba aizoides*)

A hedgehog of rigid, dark green, keeled leaves, equipped with bristles, surmounted by a leafless stem and crowded clusters of brilliant relatively large yellow flowers, the whole not more than 3 inches high: this is what you see if you can examine a single solitary plant of Yellow Whitlowgrass. More often, however, several plants grow together, their identities merged into one indeterminate pile-carpet of green. Late March is not too early.

The classic site for the plants is in the Gower peninsula on the ruins of Pennard Castle. Reports of it growing on the Pennard Cliffs date back to 1803, but it has for long been cultivated in gardens. This, and the fact that it is not native in other parts of northern Europe, has led experts, including Welsh ones, to conclude that it is a denizen – that is a species growing wild in a natural or semi-natural habitat without human assistance. This it certainly does in exposed positions on inaccessible parts of the castle walls. But it is equally at home on rocks on Pwlldu Head, south of Pennard, and further east at Nicholston Burrows, Port Eynon and Worm's Head.

Those without time or inclination for lengthy walks can see Yellow Whitlowgrass 'in the wild' by driving on from Pennard to the neighbouring village of Southgate, and taking the cliff path towards Shire Combe. Almost at once, on the left of the path, there stands a rock on which there are usually two or three plants to be admired.

AREA SIX: NORTHERN COUNTIES

1: *Derbyshire*

Cranberry (*Vaccinium oxycoccos*)

This delicate plant, with petals upswept like those of a cyclamen, may once have provided cranberry sauce, a task since assumed by the more robust American Cranberry (*Vaccinium macrocarpon*). The stems of our own wild plant, thread-like and prostrate, project stalks, at first erect, then drooping, an inch or more long. Each supports an individual flower, with a crest of pink 'plumes' and a sharp, down-pointing 'beak' of stamens which may have suggested the plant's original German name, *kranebeere*, and the original English version, Craneberry.

The leaves are dark green above and paler green beneath with edges turned down, as if to limit the amount of moisture the plant might lose. Indeed the Cranberry grows most happily on a spongy water-bed of sphagnum moss which, like the Cranberry, is itself becoming ever scarcer as more and more of the countryside is artificially drained.

Sites for the Cranberry are scattered widely across the country, except in the north of Scotland, where a closely related plant, Small Cranberry (*Vaccinium microcarpon*), is the dominant species. Wales is very well represented especially in north and central Wales, and the south of England has by no means 'gone dry'. There, there are sites in west Surrey, in north Hampshire and in Sussex, on Welches Common near Petworth (approximate grid reference 982-176). But a special distinction must go to Derbyshire, where a site near Howden Reservoir is named Cranberry Bed, and another nearby containing a number of small bogs is known as Cranberry Clough. June is probably safest in anything but a really damp season.

Jacob's Ladder (*Polemonium caeruleum*)

Even though he was not the first to find it, the tall polemonium with its peal of blue bells made a lasting impression on John Ray when he first saw it growing wild in Yorkshire, nearly three centuries ago. 'Called by the vulgar *Ladder to Heaven* and *Jacob's Ladder* [this was] found by Dr. Lister in Carleton-beck, in the falling of it into the River Air; but more plentifully both with a blue flower and a white about Malham Cove, a place so remarkable that it's esteemed one of the Wonders of Craven. It grows there in a wood on the left hand of the Water, as you go to the Cove from Malham plentifully; and also at *Cordil* or the *Wern*, a remarkable Cove, where comes out a great stream of water, near the said Malham.' (It still grows not far away.)

Even today, the true appeal of Jacob's Ladder comes as much from the remote rocks and ravines in which it sometimes grows as from the plant itself: characteristics which proclaim it as a truly native species and not a garden escape. Derbyshire is another favoured county, and many a pilgrim has been to visit Jacob's Ladder at Winnats Pass on grass too steep for the browsing sheep or at Chrome Hill in upper Dovedale. The stands of Jacob's Ladder among the grassland of Lathkill Dale show the plant in a gentler setting, more typical, perhaps, of habitats elsewhere in parts of north and central Europe. Flowers come in June and July.

2: *Lancashire*

Dark-red Helleborine (*Epipactis atrorubens*)

This species is to be sharply distinguished from the even rarer Red Helleborine, whose flowers are far fewer, paler, less ready to open. The Dark-red Helleborine, on the other hand, shows a spike perhaps 2 feet long with a dozen or more flowers, with open petals, the outer ones coloured dark red or even violet. The lower parts of the lips are green with red margins and spotted within with red. The purplish-green leaves are placed in two opposite ranks.

This plant, rightly described as very local, is most often found on limestone rocks and fine screes from Derbyshire northwards to the north coast of Scotland, where it can be found growing right by the coast in the Cape Wrath area. The rocks around Inchnadamph in Scotland are another fruitful site.

There are patches of Dark-red Helleborine in the Yorkshire Dales, particularly in Wharfedale around Grass Wood. But a more interesting setting is to be found near Silverdale in Lancashire south of Kendal, on the limestone pavement at Gait Barrows, the grid reference for which is 480–772. Here, the normal, slightly acidic content of the rain has dissolved parts of the limestone, leaving channels and pockets which prove ideal billets for the Dark-red Helleborine. This is an NCC Reserve and permits are needed by those planning to leave the public footpaths. A permit for the NCC is required also for visits to another site for the Dark-red Helleborine, Clawthorpe Fell in Cumbria. The second half of June, into July, offers chances of good flowers.

3: *North Yorkshire*

Hairy Stonecrop (*Sedum villosum*)

Two to six inches tall, this little plant stands out from its moorland surroundings like a misplaced piece of jewellery. The whole plant has a rosy glow and each petal is marked with a faint line of purple running from the base to the tip. The centre of the flower is of a darker and redder purple. The upper part of the plant, including the calyx, is covered with short hairs exuding a viscid substance. However, the word *villosum*, derived from the adjective meaning 'shaggy, with fairly long hairs', seems rather out of place here. The leaves – stalkless, fleshy, parallel-sided, flat beneath, blunt – are usually placed alternately up the stem.

Yorkshire seems the most southerly county for this species and it has been recorded on Scar Close, on the south-east side, where the ground starts to rise up towards the hills above. In general, the quickest way to discover Hairy Stonecrop is to look for any small streams or rills in the neighbourhood, and to to work down them, searching in particular for places where the water trickles down over flat stones or rocks. Hairy Stonecrop is also to be found in flushes on slopes on either side of the Pennine Way above the village of Knock, to be reached from Appleby in Cumbria. There are other sites in Lancashire, and a few in Scotland, but no permanent ones in Wales.

Some books have this species flowering as early as June; but July and August are safer.

*Lady's Slipper (*Cypripedium calceolus*)

Though it may not look the part, this is a truly native species, known to have grown wild in Helkes Wood near Ingleborough, North Yorkshire as early as 1640, if not before. Most of the past records of Lady's Slipper have come from Yorkshire, although there have been others from Castle Eden Dene in Co. Durham as well as from Cumbria.

Today the only remaining site is in Yorkshire where, on a hillside of grass and stones, a single surviving plant lives on, confined within a heavily barred and anchored cage. Whether this tragic finale is a reproach to gardeners, field botanists, sheep or rabbits, remains an open question, but we are all asked not to attempt to visit the plant, so that the soil on the slope, which is thin enough already, is not further disturbed.

Meanwhile orchid experts at the Royal Botanic Gardens, Kew are working to provide new offspring, derived wholly or in part from the wild plant, in the hope of cultivating these in a patch of wild countryside for exhibition to a wider public. One day, perhaps, when multiplied sufficiently, plants of the Lady's Slipper could be sold through garden centres so that all of us could install some in our rockeries.

Anyone who has the opportunity to see the Lady's Slipper in flower – and there are often as many as six blooms at a time – should plan the visit not later than the first week in June.

*Thistle Broomrape (*Orobanche reticulata*)

This is a handsome plant, its flowers tinged with pink and net-veined with dark purple lines. As with some other Broomrapes, only the upper flowers, newly opened, are in perfect condition.

The number of sites for this species, all in Yorkshire, can probably be counted on the fingers of one hand – partly, no doubt, because of the plant's association with thistles, unloved by farmers and gardeners alike. One – probably the safest billet for the species – is in the Ripon Parks Military Training Area, where several hundred heads have been counted in the past. This site may be approached via Headquarters, Ripon Station, Deverall Barracks, Ripon, North Yorkshire HQ4 2RB, but sponsorship for an authorised visit might be required from the Yorkshire Wildlife Trust, or from a similar conservation body.

A second site is approached from Thorner, a village 7 miles north-east of Leeds, close to quarries which may originally have been used during the Roman occupation, and on a site leased by the Yorkshire Wildlife Trust from a private owner. There is a further site at Malton, north-east of York, but the locality that has received most publicity recently lies a few miles to the north of Ferrybridge on the A1 on the slip-road signposted to Wakefield, with a smaller sign marked Aberford. Park the car, and without leaving the Aberford slip-road search the thistles on either side. Mid-July is a good time to do so.

4: *Co. Durham*

Alpine Bartsia (*Bartsia alpina*)

Alpine Bartsia is a member of a family which includes some of the more conspicuous and interesting lipped flowers: Snapdragons, Cowwheats and Foxgloves, for example. Yet the unassuming 4–6 inch Alpine Bartsia is one of the species most sought after by botanists. The flowers, the calyx and some of the upper leaves of this plant are suffused with a rich dark but somewhat subdued purple: a most distinctive rarity.

For centuries, Teesdale, in Co. Durham, one of the best sites for this species, remained relatively unexplored by botanists. The main road from Middleton-in-Teesdale accompanies the River Tees upstream only as far as Langdon Beck, and from that point onwards the river cannot be followed except along tracks and footpaths, and its source reached only by toiling over 10 miles of desolate moor on which stands the highest farm in Britain. The rainfall is also among the highest in the country. Even the great John Ray did not look for Alpine Bartsia in Teesdale but found it on the other side of the Pennine watershed near Orton in 1668.

The place to look for Alpine Bartsia in Teesdale is along the stretch of the river known locally, but seldom marked on maps, as Cetry Bank. This is reached by taking the track from Langdon Beck to Widdy Bank Farm, asking for permission to park the car there, and walking down the left bank of the river to the bend at grid reference 843-297. The site can also be reached along the Pennine Way. July and August are the best months.

*Spring Gentian (*Gentiana verna*)

Although only 1–2 inches in height the Spring Gentian, which produces brilliant blue flowers up to an inch across, each on a separate stalk, is surely Teesdale's 'Jewel in the Crown'.

The Spring Gentians usually come into flower in the third week of May, and can be seen in quantity on the sward above the Cow Green Reservoir on the left-hand side of the track leading from the car-park downhill towards the river. Fortunately there is no need to leave the track in order to admire the plants. The limestone beneath them has at one time been invaded by molten rock, which transformed it from conventional limestone into 'sugar limestone', so called because of its resemblance to coarse white sugar. It particularly suits some of our rarest species.

In earlier times Teesdale was such a secluded district that it is no surprise to learn that the Spring Gentian was first discovered elsewhere, 'in the mountains betwixt Gort and Galloway' (Galway), in or shortly before 1650.

Cow Green Reservoir is a memorial to the battle fought and lost in the 1960s against the development plans of the Tees Valley and Cleveland Water Board. Yet somewhere on the grassy slope leading to the water's edge, the rare Teesdale Violet (*Viola rupestris*) survives, though without a three-point theodolite bearing it is hard to describe just where. When found, the plant can easily be recognised: no other violet that has leaves and flowers arising from the stem has hairy leaf-stalks.

Yellow Marsh Saxifrage (*Saxifraga hirculus*)

The plant is a delight, with – usually – a lone, yellow-petalled inch-long blossom at the end of a slender stem. There are reddish hairs on the stem, reddish hairs on the sepals, and orange spots within the flower. There are probably fewer than 20 sites for this plant in the whole of the country, shared between Yorkshire, Cumbria, Midlothian and eastern Scotland.

The site we are about to consider lies within the NCC's Moor House Nature Reserve which is one of the largest in the country. It can be approached, preferably perhaps, from the Appleby side since this makes it possible to examine a grassy area on which Yellow Marsh Saxifrage often flowers – namely the slopes on the west side of the Pennine Way, uphill from the point where the road to the Silverband Mine diverges from the track leading up to the Radar Receiving Station.

The best site on the reserve, however, is reached on a bearing due east from the Radar Station. After a walk of about 2½ miles, the Moss Burn is reached and should be followed downstream towards Moor House which is visible from a fair distance away. The place to look for Yellow Marsh Saxifrage is wherever a flush of water breaks through the peat blanket bringing up with it some dissolved limestone from below. Occasionally wire enclosures are placed round growing plants to keep out sheep, and should be looked for diligently through binoculars. Do not try, though, before the beginning of August.

5: *Cumbria and Northumberland*

Alpine Enchanter's-Nightshade (*Circaea alpina*)

This is one of our rarer plants, occasionally frequent in the Lake District but seldom outside it. Once seen, it can readily be distinguished from the very common 'ordinary' Enchanter's Nightshade (*Circaea lutetiana*) but not so easily from Upland Enchanter's-Nightshade (*Circaea × intermedia*) which is a sterile hybrid between *C. alpina* and *C. lutetiana*.

Look for the following features proclaiming the true Alpine species. First, it is seldom above 6 inches in height. Second, the leaf-stalks are winged along the sides and flat (not furrowed) above. Third, the leaves are markedly heart-shaped at the base. Fourth, the petals are only shallowly notched. Fifth, the flowers are crowded together at the top of the stem and not spaced at intervals along it. This structural difference is important, because in the case of the two larger plants, the stem elongates during the flowering period thus distancing the flowers from one another. In the Alpine species the stem does not elongate until after the petals have dropped, so that in the meantime they remain in close company.

To see Alpine Enchanter's-Nightshade drive north along the west side of Ullswater, looking on the west side of the road for a lane uphill with a sign bearing the legend 'Seldom seen'. The lane leads to a house of that name, but there is no need to intrude that far. Walk uphill, looking on the left-hand side particularly in the spots where water trickles down across mossy stones. Try July and August.

May Lily (*Maianthemum bifolium*)

There has been some doubt as to whether this two-leaved miniature lily is a native species, though it is thought to be so at a locality near Harkness, 6 miles from Scarborough. This site, sometimes referred to as Forge Valley and sometimes as Cockrah Wood, lies above the River Derwent in the midst of a vast area controlled by the Forestry Commission. Some of the plants there lie on a steep slope planted with Larch, others are beneath a strip of broad-leaf trees. Opinion is divided as to how either colony can be induced to flower more regularly and how predators (?slugs, ?pheasants, ?deer, ?wood-pigeons) could be prevented from biting off the flower heads. Similar problems have beset another small colony at Allerthorpe, south-east of York – also in a wood of broad-leaf trees.

The most southerly site is in Norfolk in Swanton Novers Great Wood, south-west of Holt; this is a native wood remote from dwellings, but no claim is made that the plants there are native. The most traditional site is in the north-west of Co. Durham on the edge of a conifer wood below the village of Hunstanworth, near Stanhope. There, however, the May Lilies have proved contrary. Most of the wood in which they originally flowered was felled, but a strip close to the River Derwent was left undisturbed as a conservation measure. The plants however have disdained their sheltered accommodation and continued to flower in mid-June unprotected in the open, just where the trees had been cleared.

AREA SEVEN: SCOTLAND

*Alpine Catchfly (*Lychnis alpina*)

This little gem, as seen wild in Scotland, is barely 6 inches tall and will grow only on the peculiar rock known as serpentine, and then only if the rock becomes decomposed.

However, it is worth a long struggle to see it. Kirriemuir is the nearest town of any size to the first landmark which is Jock's Road up above Glen Doll, and the correct approach is to stay on Jock's Road until the next landmark, the Burn of Fialzioch, a tributary of the River Esk, can be clearly distinguished. This torrent, which has to be followed to its source, is marked clearly enough on maps, but in practice large parts of it are concealed from view as it foams down beneath vertical cliffs, and one has to abandon any idea of following a tow-path along its banks. The visitor should be looking for some stony rocky ground at variance with the surrounding moorland, close to, but above the source of the Burn of Fialzioch. This site is marked on maps as Meikle Kilrannoch, and has become as well known to botanists as the original site on Little Kilrannoch half a mile away to the south-west which was specified in Bentham and Hooker's *British Flora* and in *Mountain Flowers* by John Raven and Max Walters.

The unguided should take with them a map-compass. A whistle may also prove useful in an area where mist can develop unexpectedly even on days when the sun has been shining below. Try for the last week in June.

Alpine Milk-vetch (*Astragalus alpinus*)

Once you have seen this vetch, there is no mistaking it for another.
The individual flowers are variously shaded, from the keel-petals
which are dark violet to the standard or uppermost petal which is
pale blue, tipped with lilac. The remaining two side-petals, known as
the wings, are creamy. The flowers are grouped together but loosely
arranged, and pointing in no particular direction – a feature which
serves to distinguish it from the Purple Milk-vetch (*Astragalus
danicus*), as well as from Purple Oxytropis (*Oxytropis halleri*), both of
which show flowers upright, together in a tight bunch. In *Oxytropis*,
as its Latin or, rather, Greek-derived name implies, the keel is
pointed; in *Astragalus*, blunt.

There are but four known colonies of Alpine Milk-vetch, the most
exciting of which is probably the site in Glen Doll, where it has been
known for more than a century and a half. To reach this colony the
visitor must toil for some 2 miles up the glen into Jock's Road (really
a well-trodden but rough single-track path) until he sees on the left
hand a somewhat forbidding cliff, known as Craig Maud, the
approximate grid reference for which is 240-769. This is a site for
many other alpine rarities apart from the Milk-vetch, and
conservationists have recently become concerned about the numbers
of visitors there. An alternative site is on the main ridge of Ben y
Vrackie, where, however, the plants grow among grass and where it
is all too easy to tread unwittingly on the leaves. July is the month.

*Alpine Rock-cress (*Arabis alpina*)

The main attraction of this plant must surely be that it is found essentially under one rock only on the Cuillin Hills of southern Skye. In contrast to the Garden Arabis (*Arabis caucasica*), its leaves are of a sharp green (not greyish or whitish) and more deeply toothed, and the flowers are smaller (up to $\frac{3}{8}$ inch in diameter) and unscented. The gardener's plant is a native of the Mediterranean and Middle East, and is at home on a dry wall or well-drained bank; the alpine species needs a niche on a cold damp ledge, and flowers later: not usually before the first week of June.

Alpine Rock-cress was first found in Britain in 1887 by H.C. Hart while on his honeymoon in the Cuillin Hills, since when, despite the passage of more than a century, no other site has been discovered. From Sligachan, take the B8009 road and, shortly before Carbost, a hairpin turn to the left. Park at a lay-by where the road runs close to the River Brittle (approximate grid reference 420-250). Then walk along the north bank of the river and into a moderately steep slope of scree and boulders, climbing well beyond the point where there is still any river to be seen. Follow a notional projection of the river's course upwards towards a gap in the skyline, looking for a steep cliff on the right hand around which plants are to be expected.

*Alpine Sow-thistle (*Cicerbita alpina*)

The giant blue thistle, rising to a height of 6 feet or more, is certainly the most handsome of all the mountain plants which draw so many botanists to Scotland each summer. In former times it would have prospered in lightly wooded pine forests fringing the Highlands, as it does today in Scandinavia; but as these habitats disappeared from Scotland over the centuries, rocky outcrops and deep ravines – rather less suitable for the plant's needs – have become its main refuge. Meanwhile it requires a constant supply of moisture provided either by melting snow or by dams occurring fortuitously from fallen rock. Today the Alpine Sow-thistle would be seen far more often if its tender green leaves were not a temptation for the deer, and it survives largely on rocks, gullies and chimneys too precipitous for the animals to attempt to climb.

The species was first discovered in 1801 by George Don on one of the corries of Lochnagar, where it still clings on. The only other known stations are at Glen Doll in the Clova mountains, Caenlochan (where this photograph was taken), Coire Kander, south of Braemar, and at Glen Canness in Angus (where the survival of the colony remains in doubt). For the newcomer, Glen Doll may offer the best prospects since there are several different sites with possibilities, for instance on Craig Maud, the Dounault and on other ravines down which water pours to the glen below.

August is the earliest month for flowers.

Awlwort (*Subularia aquatica*)

Awlwort is seldom seen above the water level, and it seems an act of faith to grope for it in the mud around the shallow edges of some chilly mountain lochan where it likes to grow. Once found, however, the plant repays inspection. The leaves are finely pointed and almost cylindrical. They all spring from the base of the plant, and the stem, though branched, is bare except for the minute four-petalled white flowers. As might be expected, the flowers offer no nectar, and are rarely visited by insects. They are automatically self-pollinated. At 1–2 inches in height, this must be one of the smallest members of the cabbage family.

The plant grows best in waters starved of rich minerals, and many people have been taken to see it in the slaty waters of Llyn Idwal while on a visit to the other rarities of Snowdonia. It also grows as far south as Aberaeron, in Cardigan Bay, in the waters of Llyn Eiddwen. It is nevertheless more at home in Scotland, and the barer and more unpromising the loch, the more likely it is that Awlwort will be there. This particular specimen came from Coill a Choire in Aberardur Forest, about 20 miles from Kingussie, but it could have come from a dozen other such places, in late summer.

Other water plants such as Quillwort (*Isoetes*) and Shore-weed (*Littorella uniflora*) often grow in company with Awlwort, but can easily be told apart. Shore-weed has leaves which are flat on one side and rounded on the other; Quillwort has no flowers and reproduces through spores which can be seen at the base of the (often) backwardly curved leaves.

*Diapensia (*Diapensia lapponica*)

Diapensia was first discovered in Britain in July 1951 above Glenfinnan and is still known on only two sites in the British Isles, both in the Highlands. Try for the first week in June.

The cup-shaped flowers, up to $\frac{5}{8}$ inch across, are white, but reflections from the golden stamens within give them a creamy sheen. The leaves are dark green, shiny, leathery, obtuse, paddle-shaped and packed together as densely as the scales of an armadillo. *En masse*, the plants look pin-cushiony, because – although the flowers are carried individually on reddish stalks an inch high – they seem to rest on a dome of leaves, like almonds on a cake. Few illustrations show the light brown sepals beneath each flower.

There are two ways of approaching the summit of Fraoch-bheinn on which hundreds of Diapensia plants can be found in flower in early June. One is to start up the track from the western outskirts of Glenfinnan, cross the fence by the deer-gate on the left, climbing northwards, and then, at about 1000 feet, continue due west to the summit. The alternative route is to start from the village of Crook (grid reference 875-818), following the stream first north, then north-east up the Allt-an-Utha. Look for the outstandingly different area of quartz-rich rock on which the plants grow. An alternative site exists close to the main upper ridge of the mountains of the Glenquoich Forest, although the spot is less accessible and the number of flowers on show smaller. Plants of Diapensia for the garden can, according to that invaluable work *The Plant Finder*, be obtained from a Berwickshire nursery.

Irish Lady's-tresses (*Spiranthes romanzoffiana*)

Outside North America, this species, of which there may be more than one form, is known only in the British Isles. It is distinguished by the arrangement of the flowers which are in three spirally twisted rows, instead of in one only as in the other species of this genus.

Irish Lady's-tresses was discovered in south-west Ireland in the first decade of the nineteenth century, in 1892 in Northern Ireland, and in 1923 on the island of Coll in the Inner Hebrides. On the mainland, the chief site, found first by John Raven, has been at Ardnamurchan, close to Shiel Bridge, in the western Highlands. There it has appeared in a variety of sites, often where cattle or even humans have trodden during the winter: on both sides of the river-bank by the bridge itself, on a farm development at nearby Cliff, and on fields southward towards the pier, especially on land flooded in the winter. Unfortunately, though, the plant cannot be depended on to flower consistently on any one site. Land where as many as 50 plants have been on show during one season can be bare during the following year, and sometimes even the year after that.

A further discovery, this time on the English mainland, was made in 1957 by Mr and Mrs P.C. Hall and Mrs B. Welch in the Tavistock area; but here, too, there are years when no flowers are to be seen.

They appear, though sporadically, towards the end of July.

Lovage (*Ligusticum scoticum*)

Although it has been recorded from Northumberland, no one would quibble about the normal practice of describing this plant as Scots Lovage, for it loves to grow in the barest and least hospitable cliffs of the northern Highlands. There, the shining, vivid green, fretted leaves, spreading across the rocks like samples from some green tapestry, surprise even those well acquainted with the plant.

The rootstock is ribbed, and suitably stout near the base, with the lower leaves often coloured purple; the flowers are white. This is a member of the celery family and, as *livèche*, is widely used in Roman and other Continental cookery, where the young leaves, ribs and leaf-stalks are eaten like celery. However, it seems less enthusiastically welcome in Scotland, where it is said that the leaves are sometimes eaten as a pot-herb. There seems no solid justification for the botanical name *ligusticum*, meaning 'from Liguria'.

The flowering season seems relatively short, late July, in the north at least, being the most favourable 'window', but the plant is a perennial, so that if the weather is not propitious in one year the plant-hunter may meet with better luck the next time round.

The granite rocks of the north coast of Scotland – as for instance to the west of Bettyhill – offer good prospects for seeing this plant in perfect condition, and those visiting the bird sanctuaries such as Handa (facilities through the Royal Society for the Protection of Birds, Edinburgh) are often well rewarded too.

Motherwort (*Leonurus cardiaca*)

This is a stately plant, growing as high as 4 feet, with unmistakable, deeply cut leaves. The flowers, in distant whorls up the stem, are pale pink or white, spotted pink. Motherwort has enjoyed a reputation, dating from centuries BC, for relieving the pangs of childbirth and mitigating the shocks of heart attacks. So one might have expected that plants would have lingered on around the ruins of ancient monasteries and castles, the dispensaries of the past, as happened in the case of Birthwort. But it was not to be.

Motherwort is something of a mystery. On the continent of Europe it flowers from Scandinavia to Greece, also particularly around the walls of the Kremlin, and is regarded throughout as a native species. In Britain it is recorded from sites scattered over almost the whole of the country – but is classed as a casual. It is a perennial, yet frequently it does not persist. Older records in Sussex, Cornwall, Kent, Norfolk and Essex have not been sustained, though it has cropped up once more in Gloucestershire after a long absence. Coastal Wales has a fair number of sites, especially in the north.

Motherwort is most often found along verges and on waste places, and appears to benefit from the shelter of steep hedge-banks or even walls. The accompanying photograph was taken at Logierait, near Pitlochry, on the north bank of the River Tay, on the left-hand hedge of the side road proceeding uphill from the inn at Logierait. The plants have flowered on this site during July and August for several years in succession. But, with this particular species, one takes nothing for granted.

Net-leaved Willow (*Salix reticulata*)

The table-tennis-bat leaves and general habit of this shrub (a mere 6 inches high) set it apart from all our other willows. The creeping stem strikes new roots as it develops, so that the plants are often seen together *en masse*. The dark green leaves on 1-inch stalks are nearly as broad as long, with the vein structure as deeply impressed on the upper surface as the tributaries of some great river basin might be on a relief map. The leaves are pale grey beneath, and the same pattern of veins is seen there, standing out prominently from the leaf-surface. New catkins appear in June or July with the fully developed leaves.

This species was first discovered in 1777 by the Revd John Lightfoot, Chaplain to the Duchess of Portland and author of the first comprehensive Flora of Scotland. But despite the efforts of many subsequent botanists over more than 200 years, this willow has remained a rare and local plant.

The most promising areas are in the Breadalbane Mountains around Loch Tay, where on some of the more fertile cliffs it is the dominant willow. In Glen Fee, however, several other rare willows are to be found together in Corrie Sharroch (marked on 1:25 000 Pathfinder Series maps) at the southern end of the glen, on a grid reference of 255-745. On Ben Lawers Net-leaved Willow is present in quantity on rocks below but close to the summit to the east of the main ascent path.

Nootka Lupin (*Lupinus nootkatensis*)

This plant was discovered in the last decade of the eighteenth century by Archibald Menzies, Scottish naval surgeon to George Vancouver during the latter's voyage of exploration along the Pacific coast of North America. Nootka Sound is on the west coast of Vancouver Island.

Today, after nearly two centuries, the plant has returned to the wild again, appropriately in Scotland, the original home of its discoverer, and is recognised in the official Lists of British Vascular Plants prepared for the British Museum of Natural History and the Botanical Society of the British Isles. The photograph, taken near Fort William, shows the normal habitat chosen by the plant: a bank of shingle, often on an island in mid-stream. The mountain in the background is Ben Nevis, rising to the south-east of Fort William and with some snow still remaining on 8 June.

Apart from its unusual habitat, the plant can be distinguished by the number of leaflets on each 'fan' – seldom more than seven – and by the fact that the leaflets are shorter than the stalks carrying them. The flowers vary in colour from white, especially when in bud, through pink and blue, to deep purple in maturity. In the north of Scotland it is worth looking through the trees and bushes lining the bank to search for a flash of blue. There was one especially impressive site on the banks of the Dee on the road from Braemar to Ballater, but the plants appear to have subsequently moved on. The first half of June is the right time to look for the flowers at their best.

Norwegian Mugwort (*Artemisia norvegica*)

It is worth a week's hard labour to see the smiling face of this rarity, gazing like a miniature sunflower across one of the handful (some say two sites only) of sandstone boulders over which it presides. Elsewhere, it is found only in the glacial lakes of Norway or in parts of the Urals, and was not officially recorded in Britain until 1952 – two years after its original finder, Sir Christopher Cox, had unwittingly encountered it.

The whole plant is little more than an inch tall, with delicate, neatly fingered silky leaves, yet it manages to produce a solitary disc of yellow florets half an inch wide. Sometimes the disc is turned away or nodding, but this serves merely to show off the neat edging of bracts, each with a green central midrib and dark brown edging, surrounding the crush of yellow florets.

As can be seen, the plants flower in a mountains-of-the-moon wasteland of sandstone, where no one could have dreamed of planting them (and it would be a super-optimist who would expect them to grow anywhere else – in a rock-garden for instance). Nevertheless, the terrain is friable and easily disturbed, and the number of visitors must, in the interest of the plants themselves, be limited. The nearest point of contact has therefore to be the Information Centre at Knockam Cliffs and such further hints that may be available from the Inverpolly National Nature Reserve management about the slopes of Cul Mor, and points west of there. The last week in July is a good time for trying.

Pipewort (*Eriocaulon aquaticum*)

Pipewort is a vegetable curiosity – one of our rarest. The root has been described as worm-like, since it is white, jointed and tranversely furrowed. It bears a crowded array of sharp translucent sub-aqua leaves and, above them, clear of the water, a twisted and furrowed flowering stem, or scape as botanists call it. The flowers grow as a disc at the end of the scape, with male and female flowers mixed in the same heads. The outer bracts around the disc are grey, the inner black. The outer flowering segments are lead-coloured with a tuft of hairs at the tips, while the inner segments (chiefly male) carry a black gland near the top.

Pipewort is a creeping perennial and is able to form mats round the shallow edges of peaty lochs. It is known from sites in the west of Ireland, in Inverness, and within the Inner Hebrides including the Isle of Skye. One suitable site in Skye is on the road from Sligachan westwards to Drynoch where the road passes close to Loch nan Eilean at the approximate grid reference 470-350. There are other sites in shallow lochans in the Glen Sligachan area, as also on the Broadford-Armadale road further south.

This is the sole European representative of a genus that occurs elsewhere only in the case of American and East Asian species. The end of July onwards is the time to be looking.

*Purple Coltsfoot (*Homogyne alpina*)

This plant was first reported in 1813 by the Scottish botanist and nurseryman George Don, and rediscovered in Glen Clova in 1951 by another Scottish botanist, Mr A.A. Slack. Forty years on, the colony is still surviving; a score or two of plants carpet the single, undistinguished heathery ledge on which they are established and beneath which it is hoped that there will, one day, be more plants. Understandably perhaps, since the colony is so small, conservationists would prefer to limit the number of callers to zero. Misconceptions, if not plants, abound. 'Pale violet', reads one description, with the flowering period given as May to August. 'Late March to early May', says another, otherwise trustworthy, Flora which describes the flowers, with more realism, as reddish-orange. In fact, the third or fourth week of June is usually the right time to look for the flowers. The florets of Purple Coltsfoot are all tubular, upstanding in a bunch but in some disarray, like the hairs of a misused paintbrush. There are no outer strap-like ray florets, as is the case with the common yellow Coltsfoot of early spring. The colour of Purple Coltsfoot could be described as a dusky pink of the kind which John Gerard might have called 'overworn', plus some orange tints.

Whether the Purple Coltsfoot produces viable seed in Scotland or whether, as would seem probable from the disposition of the leaves, it extends itself further through an expanding root system, is a matter for speculation.

Purple Oxytropis (*Oxytropis halleri*)

Bettyhill, a village on Scotland's north coast, was founded originally to accommodate the crofters and small farmers evicted during the eighteenth-century 'clearances' from their holdings in Strathnaver at a time when landlords found it more profitable to run sheep than tenants. It was named after Elizabeth, Countess of Sutherland.

Today Bettyhill offers salmon fishing and a fine sandy beach. Botanists, however, prefer to visit the headland behind which the village shelters from the storms of the north. There, on the grassy banks between the boulders, blooms the Purple Oxytropis, one of the most alluring members of the Pea-flower family. The flowers, carried on upright stems nearly nine inches tall, and longer than the leaves, are vivid red, turning later to purple. Close examination of the flowers reveals that the lowest petals, forming the keel, end in a point, one of the features distinguishing it from the lowland Purple Milk-vetch (*Astragalus danicus*). Each leaf carries some ten pairs of closely-packed leaflets.

Bettyhill is by no means the only site for the Purple Oxytropis. One alternative is the mountain of Ben Vrackie to the north of Pitlochry, involving a relatively gentle ascent, past the Loch a Choire to the summit at about 2700 feet. A search along the near side of the top ridge should prove productive. Early June is the safest time to visit both these stations, though some books allow a good deal more latitude.

Scottish Primrose (*Primula scotica*)

This is a distinct species, and not merely a smaller form of the Bird's-eye Primrose (*Primula farinosa*). The latter has leaves lightly scalloped round the edges, and the flowers are rose-coloured with wedge-shaped petals that are separated from each other. It is not confined to Scotland and flourishes over most of Europe. The Scottish Primrose, on the other hand, is unique to Scotland, has purplish flowers with petals not separated from one another, and the leaves are not scalloped round the edges.

The two most northerly 'counties' of the Scottish mainland namely Caithness in the east, and Sutherland in the west, are the headquarters of the Scottish Primrose. There it grows in short turf along the cliffs in some of the most exposed sites, as for instance in the Nature Conservancy Council Reserve at Invernaver to the west of Bettyhill – not the most accessible site for the visitor, but the plants can easily be found wherever flushes seep through the sand. The village of Scrabster in the crook of Thurso Bay, and the grassy slopes above it, are more easily approached and have long been a traditional site for the Scottish Primrose. At the western end of the north coast there is another spectacular site along the grassy cliffs to the west of Balnakeil near Durness, though some of this territory has been surrendered to golfers.

There are usually two periods of flowering, the first in June and July and the second in August when, often enough, the flowers are more plentiful.

Serrated Wintergreen (*Orthilia secunda*)

This rare Alpine of the wetter Highland rocks and ledges does indeed possess saw-toothed leaves which tell it apart from our other four Wintergreen species. But its really distinctive feature is surely the arrangement of the flowers in a singly oriented row along the stem. *Secundus* is the adjective used in botanical Latin to express this particular type of inflorescence, and was the one applied by Linnaeus himself to the species. The alternative vernacular name for the plant, the Yavering Bells, is certainly more picturesque, though not readily identifiable among serious campanologists.

This is a late-comer in the botanical calendar and not to be expected before mid-July. The flowers, pale green, are carried on a leafless stalk, 3–6 inches long, and are at their best only for a short while after opening. They can normally be seen on the upper slopes of the Morrone Birkwood above Braemar, in the pinewoods about Aviemore (particularly in the Craigellachie Reserve), and on the slopes of Caenlochan Glen, to the north of the main cleft. Another traditional site is on the banks of the Findhorn River, and, on Tayside, Serrated Wintergreen can also be looked for in the woods around Keltney Burn. It has been recorded in Wales on some of the stiffer slopes, including Craig Cerrig-gleisiad in Brecon, though in these more southerly regions the plant may be in flower as early as April.

Sibbaldia (*Sibbaldia procumbens*)

This little plant has a place in the history of Scotland, for it was named after Sir Richard Sibbald (1641–1722), President of the Edinburgh Royal College of Physicians and Physician to King Charles II. The name was chosen by Linnaeus.

This diminutive member of the Rose 'family' grows from a prostrate branching, woody stock, and produces flowering stems and basal leaves, rarely as much as 3 inches high. The leaves are greyish or bluish-green and the leaflets, in groups of three, terminate bluntly with an edging of three teeth, features which distinguish it from its cousins the smaller *Potentillas*. The petals, when present, are small and narrow. Often, however, none are produced and all that can then be seen of the flower are the sepals, green-with-purple, and beneath them an outer calyx of narrower 'episepals', which together give the impression of a totally green flower.

This is a plant which grows best in places where there is prolonged snow-cover and is thus seldom seen in England. In Scotland it is to be sought on ledges, in crevices or on scree, where loose detritus has been eroded from the rock-face. Many corries on the Cairn Gorm fulfil these requirements, as do other parts of mountains in Angus and the central Highlands. But the best-known site is on Ben Lawers, where plants are to be found on scree beneath, but slightly to the north of the summit, close to a grid reference, in round figures, of 640-420. The exposed chalk slopes on the Cairnwell, south of Braemar, form another fruitful site. July into August is the flowering time.

Single-flowered Wintergreen (*Moneses uniflora*)

The English name explains everything, for the plant retains its green leaves throughout the winter, and produces a single white bloom – a rather splendid saucer-shaped one, more than half an inch across, from the centre of which grows a pale green column, the style.

The alternative vernacular name for the plant, St Olaf's Candlestick, is less explicit, particularly since the 'candle', as in the photograph, invariably points to the ground during the later stages of flowering. Olaf, an eleventh-century king of the Norwegians, was posthumously beatified in 1164 after a life which had been anything but saintly. Could the reversed candle have been a mark of respect similar to the reversed arms to be seen at military funerals? More probably, it symbolised the battle of Stiklestadt in which Olaf lost his life. This was fought on 29 July 1020 during a total eclipse of the sun, when Olaf's candlestick would have been as ineffective as if it had been inverted.

There are perhaps a dozen sites for the Single-flowered Wintergreen in the east of Scotland in Snab Wood near Dyke, in pinewoods at Castle Grant, Grantown-on-Spey and in the Culbin Forest, but the best-known is in a small privately owned pinewood not far from Golspie. (Restricted entry permits are usually obtainable in advance from the nearby office of the Sutherland Estate.) The plants can be admired without leaving the main track which passes through this wood. Mid-June would be the right time to be there.

Trailing Azalea (*Loiseleuria procumbens*)

This is a ground-hugging under-shrub with a somewhat disorderly woody structure and leathery leaves which outlast the Highland winter, perhaps because their drip-dry shape helps to dislodge the raindrops and snow. *Loiseleuria*'s relationship with the Rhododendron-Azalea 'family' is a close one, the main difference – apart from mere size – being that the leaves of *Loiseleuria* grow opposite one another in pairs, whereas those of the Rhododendrons and their like are alternate.

The flowers of *Loiseleuria* are funnel-shaped, and up to $\frac{1}{4}$ inch in diameter, bright red in bud, but fading later to delicate pink and ultimately to white. The anthers, seen from a distance, suggest that the flower has a dark red centre. Though the flowering season is fairly lengthy, stretching from May into July, the individual flowers are less durable, and the petals fall away rather soon.

Despite its modest size, Trailing Azalea is not easily overlooked if only because it flowers on bare rock where almost nothing else can flourish, and because the leaves, arranged in mass formation, inhibit competition from rivals. As a member of the Heath 'tribe', Trailing Azalea prefers an acid soil, and is thus very much at home in the Cairngorms. Those with little time to spare can seek it on the rocky area around the Caernwell (height 3027 feet) south of Braemar, on grid reference 135-773, which is conveniently reached, even in summer, on a ski-tow. Further north, where it is colder, the plant can prosper at lower heights.

Water Lobelia (*Lobelia dortmanna*)

This is surely one of the frailer survivors among our rarer plants. The stemless, hollow leaves never reach the fresh air, but grow in rosettes beneath water. The flowering stems of the plants are leafless and hollow, and the flowers, in unbranched stalks rising some 6 inches above the waters, are pale and unsubstantial, nodding gracefully even when they should be at rest. Each flower consists of two lips which appear white at first sight, but on further examination show faint traces of lilac and, in the throat of the flower, a splash of bluish lavender. The upper lip is divided into two-recurved crescents, and the lower into three blunt, spreading lobes.

Water Lobelia grows in sheltered lakes and pools with shallow stony bottoms, particularly those with acid water, and under suitable conditions can occupy a considerable section of the pool, allowing the plants to be seen from a distance. It is found in Wales as far south as Glamorgan, but also on Cwm Idwal on the threshold of Snowdon, as well as on Tayside and in the Highlands of Scotland.

Late July and August is the flowering time. The plants are perennial and self-pollinating.

Yellow Oxytropis (*Oxytropis campestris*)

Here is an enchanting creamy-flowered, silvery-leaved, vetch-like plant, for which the best-known site is in Glen Clova to the north of Kirriemuir. But a car takes you no further than the Mountain Rescue Post at Glen Doll Lodge, and you are then faced with a choice of three trails.

To the right, hardy hill-climbers can begin an ascent which would ultimately take them to Ballater. Plant-hunters can afford to disregard this. In the centre of the picture is Glen Doll, which would finally bring the traveller to Braemar, and to the left is Glen Fee, which is the correct track for this particular rarity.

The first part of the journey leads through a rock-strewn pinewood, giving access over an A-shaped deer-ladder on to an open amphitheatre of marshes and rocks with, at the far end, a spectacular waterfall. From the foot of this waterfall and looking directly away from it and straight down the glen, there is on the left hand a steep slope, the nearer part of which consists of rocky moorland. Further on, however, there is an area of rock and scree, part of which has become noticeably discoloured to dark ochre, contrasting sharply with the surrounding grey. The rocks at the head of this particular section serve as the headquarters for Yellow Oxytropis, and can be most conveniently reached by traversing up along the sheep-tracks from the foot of the waterfall. An ascent from directly below the plants is not recommended. Early July is about right.

Envoi

A Conservation Code devised by the Botanical Society of the British Isles includes some good suggestions for photographers. The Society advises photographers to:

1. Watch your step. It is all too easy to step unwittingly on seedlings not yet in flower and therefore not easily distinguishable.
2. Treading on the soil may compact it, preventing water reaching seedlings of growing plants. (It is especially damaging in marshy habitats.)
3. When visiting a rare plant, avoid leaving any evidence which might betray its existence – such as taking a direct path to it, or trampling down the vegetation around it. Cover your traces by restoring the vegetation to its original posture.

   'Gardening', i.e. getting rid of vegetation which obscures the camera's view can also put rarities at risk. Live grass etc. should be tied together lightly rather than cut away, and released again as soon as the picture has been taken.
4. If possible stand while taking a photograph rather than kneel, and kneel rather than lie. Use a long-distance lens if there are likely to be seedlings around.
5. Avoid telling the world – particularly if you have found a rare plant yourself. Let the local Conservation Trust know so that they can see it is protected.
6. Take care that your photograph does not contain give-away clues as to the whereabouts of rarities – particularly on mountain ranges such as Snowdon where well-known peaks – not to speak of the Snowdon railway itself – are easily identifiable. Power-line pylons and lochs are another give-away, particularly in the Highlands.

Appendix

List of Nature Conservation Trusts in the United Kingdom associated with the Royal Society for Nature Conservation (RSNC).

AVON
Bristol 0272 268018/265490

Avon Wildlife Trust
The Old Police Station, 32 Jacob's Wells Road, Bristol. BS8 1DR

BEDS & HUNTS
Bedford 0234 64213

Bedfordshire & Huntingdonshire Wildlife Trust
Priory Country Park, Barkers Lane, Bedford. MK41 9SH

BERKS, BUCKS & OXON
Oxford 0865 775476

Berkshire, Buckinghamshire & Oxon Naturalists' Trust (BBONT)
3 Church Cowley Road, Rose Hill, Oxford. OX4 3JR

BIRMINGHAM
Birmingham 021 666 7474

Urban Wildlife Group (Birmingham), (UWG)
Unit 213, Jubilee Trade Centre, 130 Pershore St., Birmingham. B5 6ND

BRECKNOCK (Brecon)
Brecon 0874 5708

Brecknock Wildlife Trust
Lion House, 7 Lion Street, Brecon, Powys. LD3 7AY

CAMBRIDGESHIRE
Cambridge 0223 880788

Cambridgeshire Wildlife Trust
5 Fulbourn Manor, Manor Walk, Fulbourn, Cambridge. CB1 5BN

CHESHIRE
Northwich 0606 781868

Cheshire Conservation Trust
Marbury Country Park, Northwich, Cheshire. CW9 6AT

CLEVELAND
Stockton-on-Tees 0642 608405

Cleveland Wildlife Trust
The Old Town Hall, Mandale Rd, Thornaby, Cleveland. TS17 6AW

CORNWALL
Truro 0872 73939

Cornwall Trust for Nature Conservation
Five Acres, Allet, Truro, Cornwall. TR4 9DJ

CUMBRIA
Ambleside 0966 32476

Cumbria Wildlife Trust
Church St., Ambleside, Cumbria. LA22 0BU

DERBYSHIRE
Derby 0332 756610

Derbyshire Wildlife Trust
Elvaston Castle Country Park, Derby. DE7 3EP

DEVON
Exeter 0392 79244

Devon Wildlife Trust
35 New Bridge Street, Exeter, Devon. EX3 4AH

DORSET
Bournemouth 0202 24241

Dorset Trust for Nature Conservation
39 Christchurch Road, Bournemouth, Dorset, BH1 3NS

DURHAM
Durham 091 386 9797

Durham Wildlife Trust
52 Old Elvet, Durham. DH1 3HN

DYFED
Haverfordwest 0437 5462

Dyfed Wildlife Trust
7 Market Street, Haverfordwest, Dyfed. SA61 1NF

ESSEX
Rowhedge 020628 678

Essex Naturalists' Trust
Fingringhoe Wick Nature Reserve, Fingringhoe, Colchester, Essex. CO5 7DN

GLAMORGAN
Bridgend 0656 724100

Glamorgan Wildlife Trust
Nature Centre, Fountain Road, Tondu, Mid Glamorgan. CF32 0EH

GLOUCESTERSHIRE
Stonehouse 045 382 2761

Gloucestershire Trust for
Nature Conservation
Church House, Standish,
Stonehouse, Glos. GL10 3EU

GUERNSEY
Guernsey 0481 25093

La Société Guernesiaise (LSG)
c/o F. G. Caldwell, Candie
Gardens, St Peter Port,
Guernsey, C.I.

GWENT
Monmouth (9am–1pm) 0600 5501

Gwent Wildlife Trust
16 White Swan Court,
Church Street, Monmouth,
Gwent. NP5 3BR

HANTS & ISLE OF WIGHT
Romsey 0794 513786

Hampshire & Isle of Wight
Naturalists' Trust
71 The Hundred, Romsey,
Hants. SO5 8BZ

HEREFORD
Hereford 0432 356872

Herefordshire Nature Trust
Community House, 25 Castle
Street, Hereford. HR1 2NW

HERTS & MIDDX
St Albans 0727 58901

Hertfordshire & Middlesex
Wildlife Trust
Grebe House, St Michael's
Street. St Albans, Herts. AL3
4SN

KENT
Maidstone 0622 53017/59017

Kent Trust for Nature
Conservation
The Annexe, 1a Bower
Mount Road, Maidstone,
Kent. ME16 8AX

LANCASHIRE
Preston 0772 324129

Lancashire Trust for Nature
Conservation
The Pavilion, Cuerden Park
Wildlife Centre, Shady Lane,
Bamber Bridge, Preston,
Lancs. PR5 6AU

LEICESTER & RUTLAND
Leicester 0533 553904

Leicestershire & Rutland Trust for Nature
Conservation, 1 West Street, Leicester. LE1 6UU

LINCS & STH HUMBERSIDE
Alford 05212 3468

Lincolnshire & Sth Humberside Trust for Nature Conservation, The Manor House, Alford, Lincs. LN13 9DL

LONDON
London 01 278 6612/3

London Wildlife Trust
80 York Way, London. N1 9AG

MAN (ISLE OF)
Sulby 062489 7611

Manx Nature Conservation Trust
Ballamoar House, Ballaugh, Isle of Man.

MONTGOMERY
Newtown 0686 624751

Montgomeryshire Wildlife Trust
8 Severn Square, Newtown, Powys. SY16 2AG

NORFOLK
Norwich 0603 625540

Norfolk Naturalists' Trust
72 Cathedral Close, Norwich, Norfolk. NR1 4DF

NORTHAMPTONSHIRE
Northampton 0604 405285

Northants Wildlife Trust
Lings House, Billing Lings, Northampton. NN3 4BE

NORTHUMBERLAND
Durham 091 232 0038

Northumberland Wildlife Trust
Hancock Museum, Barras Bridge, Newcastle-upon-Tyne. NE2 4PT

NORTH WALES
Bangor 0248 351541

North Wales Wildlife Trust
376 High Street, Bangor, Gwynedd. LL57 1YE

NOTTINGHAMSHIRE
Nottingham 0602 588242

Nottinghamshire Wildlife Trust
310 Sneinton Dale, Nottingham. NG3 7DN

RADNORSHIRE
Llandrindod Wells 0597 3298

Radnorshire Wildlife Trust
1 Gwalia Annexe, Ithon
Road, Llandrindod Wells,
Powys, LD1 6AS

SCOTLAND
Edinburgh 031 226 4602

Scottish Wildlife Trust, (SWT)
25 Johnston Terrace,
Edinburgh. EH1 2NH

SHROPSHIRE
Shrewsbury 0743 241691

Shropshire Wildlife Trust
St George's Primary School,
Frankwell, Shrewsbury,
Shropshire. SY3 8JP

SOMERSET
Kingston St Mary 0823451 587/8

Somerset Trust for Nature
Conservation
Fyne Court, Broomfield,
Bridgwater, Somerset. TA5
2EQ

STAFFORDSHIRE
Sandon 088 97 534

Staffordshire Nature
Conservation Trust
Coutts House, Sandon,
Staffordshire. ST18 0DN

SUFFOLK
Saxmundham 0728 603765

Suffolk Wildlife Trust
Park Cottage, Saxmundham,
Suffolk. IP17 1DQ

SURREY
Guildford 0483 797575

Surrey Wildlife Trust
The Old School, School Lane,
Pirbright, Woking, Surrey.
GU24 0JN

SUSSEX
Brighton 0273 492630

Sussex Wildlife Trust
Woods Mill, Shoreham Road,
Henfield, West Sussex. BN5
9SD

ULSTER
Belfast 0232 612235

Ulster Wildlife Trust
Barnett's Cottage, Barnett
Demesne, Malone Road,
Belfast. BT9 5PB

WARWICKSHIRE
Warwick 0926 496848

Warwickshire Nature
Conservation Trust,
(WARNACT)
Montague Road, Warwick.
CV34 5LW

WILTSHIRE
Devizes 0380 5670

Wiltshire Trust for Nature
Conservation
19 High Street, Devizes,
Wiltshire. SN10 1AT

WORCESTERSHIRE
Droitwich 0905 773031

Worcestershire Nature
Conservation Trust
Hanbury Road, Droitwich,
Worcestershire. WR9 7DU

YORKSHIRE
York 0904 659570

Yorkshire Wildlife Trust
10 Toft Green, York. YO1 1JT

RSNC
Lincoln 0522 752326
595325 (Fax)

Royal Society for Nature
Conservation, (RSNC)
The Green, Nettleham,
Lincoln. LN2 2NR

RSNC is the national association of the Nature Conservation Trusts.

Select Bibliography

ALLEN, DAVID ELLISTON, *The Botanists*. (St. Paul's Bibliographies, 1986)

ANTHONY. JOHN, *John Anthony's Flora of Sutherland*, (Botanical Society of Edinburgh, 1976)

ARBER, AGNES, *Herbals*, (Cambridge University Press, 1986)

BENTHAM, GEORGE, HOOKER, SIR J.D., RENDLE, A.B., *Handbook of the British Flora*, (Reeve & Co. Ltd., Ashford, 1945)

BEVIS, J., KETTELL, R., SHEPARD, B. *Flora of the Isle of Wight*, (Isle of Wight Natural History & Archaeological Society, 1978)

BLAMEY, MARJORIE, and GREY-WILSON, CHRISTOPHER, *The Illustrated Flora of Britain and Northern Europe* (Hodder & Stoughton, 1989)

Botanical Society of the British Isles, *The Botanical Exploration of the British Isles*: Conference Report No.20. (Scottish Natural History Library, 1986)

BRADSHAW, M.E., *The Natural History of Upper Teesdale*, (Durham County Conservation Trust, 1976)

BUTCHER, ROGER W. (text), STRUDWICK, FLORENCE E. (illustrations), *Further Illustrations of British Plants*, (Reeve & Co. Ltd, Ashford, 1930)

BUTCHER, R.W., *Illustrated British Flora*, (Leonard Hill, 1961)

CHURCH, JUDITH, *Guidelines for Rare Plant Wardening*, (Conservation Association of Botanical Societies, 1988)

CLAPHAM, A.R., TUTIN, T.G., WARBURG, E.F., *Flora of the British Isles*, (Cambridge University Press, 1962)

COOMBES, ALLEN J., *Dictionary of Plant Names*, (Collingridge, 1986)

DANDY, J.E., *List of British Vascular Plants*, (Trustees of the British Museum, 1982)

DONY, J.G., PERRING, F.H., ROB, C.M., *English Names of Wild Flowers*, (The Botanical Society of the British Isles, 1980)

ELLIS, R.G., *Flowering Plants of Wales*, (National Museum of Wales, 1983)

ETTLINGER, D.M. TURNER, *British & Irish Orchids*, (Macmillan, 1976)

ewen, a.h., prime, c.t., *Ray's Flora of Cambridgeshire*, (Wheldon & Wesley, 1975)

FITCH, W.H., SMITH, W.G., *Illustrations of the British Flora*, (Reeve & Co., London, 1887)

FITTER, ALASTAIR, *Collins New Generation Guide to the Wild Flowers of Britain and Northern Europe*, (Collins, 1987)

FITTER, R.S.R., FITTER, ALASTAIR, BLAMEY, MARJORIE, *The Wild Flowers of Britain and Northern Europe* (Collins, 1979)

FITTER, R.S.R., *Finding Wild Flowers* (Collins, 1973)

GARRARD, IAN, (illustrations), STREETER, DAVID, (text) *The Wild Flowers of the British Isles*, (Macmillan, 1983)

GILMOUR, JOHN, WALTERS, MAX, *Wild Flowers*, (Collins, 1973)

GOOD, RONALD, *A Concise Flora of Dorset*, (The Dorset Natural History and Archaeological Society, 1984)

GRIGSON, GEOFFREY, *The Englishman's Flora*, (Phoenix House,1987)

HALL, P.C., *Sussex Plant Atlas*, (Booth Museum of Natural History, Brighton Borough Council, 1980)

HASLAM, SYLVIA, SINKER, CHARLES, WOLSELEY, PAT, *British Water Plants*, (Field Studies Council, 1982)

HENREY, BLANCHE, *British Botanical and Horticultural Literature before 1800* (Oxford University Press, 1975)

HOLLAND, S.C., CADDICK, H.M., DUDLEY-SMITH, D.S., *Supplement to the Flora of Gloucestershire*, (Grenfell Publications, 1986)

HYWEL-DAVIES, JEREMY, THOM, VALERIE, *The Macmillan Guide to Britain's Nature Reserves*, (Macmillan, 1984)

INGLIS, BESSIE DARLING (ed.), *Ben Lawers and its alpine Flowers*, (The National Trust for Scotland, 1972)

INGRAM, RUTH, NOLTIE, HENRY J., *The Flora of Angus*, (Dundee Museum & Art Galleries, 1981)

IVIMEY-COOK, R.B., *Atlas of the Devon Flora*, (The Devonshire Association, 1984)

JERMYN, STANLEY, T., *Flora of Essex*, (Essex Naturalists' Trust, 1974)

JOHNSON, A.T., SMITH, H.A., *Plant Names Simplified*, (Collingridge, 1931)

LANG, DAVID, *Orchids of Britain*, (Oxford University Press, 1980)

LEES, F. ARNOLD, *The Vegetation of Craven in Wharfedale*, (T. Buncle & Co., Arbroath, 1939)

—*The Flora of West Yorkshire*, (E.P. Publishing Ltd., Wakefield)

LESLIE, A.C., *Flora of Surrey-Supplement and Checklist*, (A.C. & P. Leslie, Guildford, 1987)

LOUSLEY, J.E., *Flora of Surrey*, (David & Charles, 1976)

—*Flora of the Isles of Scilly*, (David & Charles, Newton Abbot, 1971)

—*Wild Flowers of Chalk and Limestone*, (Collins, 1971)

MCCLINTOCK, DAVID, *Companion to Flowers*, (George Bell & Sons, 1966)

MCCLINTOCK, DAVID, FITTER, R.S.R., *Collins Pocket Guide to Wild Flowers*, (Collins, 1974)

MARGETTS, L. & DAVID, R.W., *A Review of the Cornish Flora*, (Institute of Cornish Studies, 1981)

MEIKLE, R.D., *Willows and Poplars of Great Britain and Ireland*, (Botanical Society of the British Isles, 1984)

MURRAY, C.W., BIRKS, H.J.B., *The Botanist in Skye*, (Botanical Society of the British Isles, 1980)

PERRING, F.H., *Hints on the Determination of Critical Groups in the British Flora*, (Botanical Society of the British Isles, 1962)

—with FARRELL, L., *British Red Data Books: Vascular Plants*, (Royal Society for Nature Conservation, 1983)

—with SELL, P.D. and WALTERS, S.M., *A Flora of Cambridgeshire*, (Cambridge University Press, 1964)

PETCH, DR C.P., SWANN, E.L., *Flora of Norfolk*, (Jarrold, 1968)

PHILIP, CHRIS, *The Plant Finder*, (Hardy Plant Society, Whitbourne, 1988)

PHILP, ERIC G., *Atlas of the Kent Flora*, (Kent Field Club, 1982)

RAVEN, JOHN, WALTERS, MAX, *Mountain Flowers*, (Collins, 1965)

RAY, JOHN, *Synopsis Methodica Stirpium Britannicarum (1724)*, (Ray Society, 1973)

RICH, MATTHEW, RICH, TIM, *Plant Crib*, (Botanical Society of the British Isles, 1988)

ROE, R.G.B., *The Flora of Somerset*, (Somerset Archaeological and Natural History Society, 1981)

ROSE, FRANCIS, *The Wild Flower Key*, (Frederick Warne, 1981)

ROUSSEAU, J.-J., *Botany – A Study of Pure Curiosity*, (Michael Joseph, 1979)

SHEPARD, B., *Supplement to The Flora of the Isle of Wight*, (Isle of Wight Natural History & Archaeological Society, 1983)

SIMPSON, FRANCIS, W., *Simpson's Flora of Suffolk*, (Suffolk Naturalists' Society, 1982)

SMITH, A.E., *A Nature Reserves Handbook*, (The Royal Society for Nature Conservation, 1982)

STEARN, WILLIAM T., *Botanical Latin*, (David & Charles, 1989)

SUGDEN, ANDREW, *Longman Illustrated Dictionary of Botany*, (Longman, 1984)

SUMMERHAYES, V.S., *Wild Orchids of Britain*, (Collins, 1969)

TOOTHILL, ELIZABETH, *Penguin Dictionary of Botany*, (Penguin Books, 1984)

TURNER, WILLIAM, *Libellus de Re Herbaria (1538)*, (The Ray Society, 1965)

TUTIN, T.G., *Umbellifers of the British Isles*, (Botanical Society of the British Isles, 1980)

WEBB, NIGEL, *Heathlands*, (Collins, 1986)

WEBSTER, MARY MCCALLUM, *Flora of Moray, Nairn and East Inverness*, (Aberdeen University Press, 1978)

WIGGINTON, M.J., GRAHAM, G.G., *Guide to the Identification of some of the more difficult Vascular Plant species*, (Nature Conservancy Council, 1981)

WOLLEY-DOD, A.H., *Flora of Sussex*, (Kenneth Saville, Hastings, 1937)

YOUNG, ANDREW, *The Prospect of Flowers*, (Viking, 1985)

Index

361

363